MW01104594

Grand Canyon Guide
Your Complete Guide to the Grand Canyon

Bruce Grubbs

Bright Angel Press
Flagstaff, Arizona

Grand Canyon Guide: Your Complete Guide to the Grand Canyon

Updated February 2012

Bright Angel Press

Flagstaff, Arizona

www.BrightAngelPress.com

ISBN-10: 0982713053

ISBN-13: 9780982713051

Contents

Acknowledgments

Thank you to all my hiking companions over the years, and especially to Art Christiansen and Jim Haggart, for putting up with my photography in the canyon. And warm thanks to Duart Martin for her unflagging support of my writing projects.

Introduction

In the Grand Canyon, Arizona has a natural wonder which is in kind absolutely unparalleled throughout the rest of the world. I want to ask you to keep this great wonder of nature as it now is... Leave it as it is. You can not improve on it. The ages have been at work on it, and man can only mar it. What you can do is to keep it for your children, your children's children, and for all who come after you, as one of the great sights which every American if he can travel at all should see. - Theodore Roosevelt

This book is designed to complement the companion website, www.GrandCanyonGuide.net . The website has much of the same information, but as it is a website, I am able to update it more frequently. Although I provide many links within the book, all the links in the book, and many more, are on the website.

Grand Canyon Guide has two major parts: Activities covers how to get to the Grand Canyon and what do do once you're there. Exploring The Canyon is for those who want to learn more about the national park, national monument, national forest, and Indian reservations that all have a part in managing the lands of the Grand Canyon region. You can also learn more about the natural and human history of the Grand Canyon.

The Canyon

- Length: 277 miles

- Width: 10 to 18 miles

- Average Depth: 1 mile

- Elevation at Colorado River: 2,000 feet

- Elevation at North Rim: 8,200 feet

These are just numbers which cannot do justice to the reality of Grand Canyon. That reality often first strikes visitors as they walk to the edge of the canyon at one of the rim viewpoints. For others, their first view is from a tour airplane or helicopter. Still others see the Grand Canyon from a float trip down the Colorado River.

For most people, the first impression of the Grand Canyon is of an utterly alien landscape. But if you spend some time at the Canyon, slowly the landscape will start to make sense. First of all, you'll see that the Grand Canyon is far more than a single canyon. Instead, it is a seeming maze of side canyons, large and small. Look closer, and you'll see that the pattern is not one of chaos, but instead part of an underlying order- an order enforced by the demands of flowing water and gravity.

Not so obvious are the effects of mountain building forces that lifted the Colorado Plateau high above sea level. These same forces created the Rocky Mountains and provided the headwaters for one of the continent's largest rivers, the Colorado, which in turn, gave the river the power to carve immense canyons from the Colorado Plateau.

The result is the Grand Canyon of the Colorado River that we see today. But the Grand Canyon is far more than a piece of scenery or a diorama-like view to be glanced at and then discarded. It is a place, a unique portion of the Earth that is a living, breathing ecosystem. If you'll give it some of your time, the Grand Canyon will reward you with some insights into its two billion year history.

Map Legend

)(	Pass		═══(17)═══	Interstate Highway
▲	Peak		═══(89)(64)═══	US/State Highway
Spring	Spring		═══════	Local Road
Rapids	Rapids		──────	Gravel Road
P	Parking		= = = = =	Unmaintained Road
Shuttle Bus	Shuttle Bus Stop		▪ ▪ ▪ ▪ ▪ ▪	Featured Trail
Lodge	Lodge		· · · · · · · ·	Other Trail
Campground	Campground		──────	River or Creek
Trailer Camping	Trailer Camping		── ── ── ──	Intermittent Stream
Trailer Dump	Trailer Dump Site			
Showers	Showers			
Backcountry	Backcountry Campsite			
Picnic	Picnic Area			
Visitor Center	Visitor Center			
Ranger Station	Ranger Station			
▪	Point of Interest			
Viewpoint	Viewpoint			

Activities: Things to Do

Getting There

We simply need that wild country available to us, even if we never do more than drive to its edge and look in. For it can be a means of reassuring ourselves of our sanity as creatures, a part of the geography of hope. - Wallace Stegner

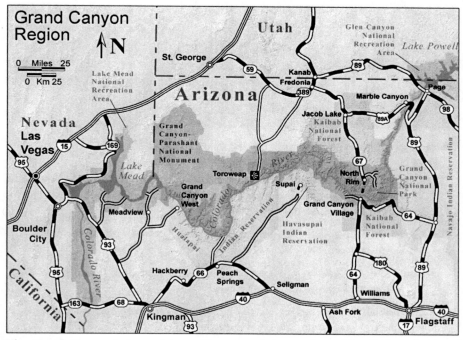

The Grand Canyon is located in northwestern Arizona, about 80 miles northwest of Flagstaff, Arizona, and about 150 miles southeast of St. George, Utah. Although access to the North Rim of the Grand Canyon is often made from Utah, the entire Grand Canyon lies within the state of Arizona.

Public Transportation

Public transportation to and around the Grand canyon is limited. To reach any point other than Grand Canyon Village on the South Rim, North Rim Village, and Grand Canyon West, you'll need a car.

- Scheduled airlines serve Flagstaff, Prescott, and Kingman, Arizona, and St. George, Utah. Visitors may also fly into the major airline hubs at Las Vegas, Nevada, and Phoenix, Arizona. Air tour and air charter services are available to

3

Driving across Navajo Bridge

Grand Canyon National Park Airport at the South Rim and Grand Canyon West Airport on the southwest rim. I suggest using a flight search site such as kayak.com to check availability.

- Amtrak serves Flagstaff, Williams, and Kingman, Arizona with rail service. www.Amtrak.com, 800-872-7245

- Grand Canyon Railway offers service between Williams and Grand Canyon Village. www.thetrain.com, 800-THE-TRAIN

- Greyhound provides bus service to Flagstaff and Kingman, Arizona, Las Vegas, Nevada, and St. George, Utah. www.greyhound.com, 800-231-2222

- Arizona Shuttle offers ground shuttle service from Phoenix Sky Harbor Airport to Sedona, Flagstaff, and Grand Canyon Village on the South Rim. www.arizonashuttle.com, 877-226-8060

- Trans Canyon Shuttle offers ground shuttle service between Grand Canyon Village, Marble Canyon, and North Rim Village. www.trans-canyonshuttle.com, 928-638-2820

Rental Cars

Rental cars are available in Las Vegas, Nevada, St. George, Utah, and Page, Flagstaff, Kingman, Prescott, and Phoenix, Arizona.

Driving Directions

South Rim

Road access to Grand Canyon Village and the South Rim is from Flagstaff and Williams along I-40 and US 89 from Cameron. Since there are three highways to the South Rim, consider doing a loop drive. For example, you could go to the South Rim from Williams via AZ 64, or Flagstaff via US 180, drive Desert View Drive, and then return through Cameron and south on US 89. From US 89, turn left on the Wupatki National Momument Road, which loops past Wupatki National Monument, with its native ruins, and Sunset Crater Volcano National Monument- the most recent volcano in the Grand Canyon area.

- From Williams, drive 63 miles north on Arizona 64 to the South Rim Entrance Station.
- From Flagstaff, drive 81 miles north via US 180 and Arizona 64 to the South Rim Entrance Station.
- From Cameron, drive 55 miles west on Arizona 64 and Desert View Drive to Grand Canyon Village.

Tips for Getting Around the South Rim

Use the Free Shuttles

From March through October, roads and parking in the Grand Canyon Village area are congested. The best way to get around the village is via the free shuttle buses, which operate year-round in the village and to the Kaibab Trailhead and Yaki Point, and seasonally along Hermit Road and to Tusayan and the airport.

Park Away From the Rim

It is easiest to find a parking spot near the Backcountry Information Center at the west end of the village, or near Park Headquarters at the east end of the village. There are also large parking lots at Market Plaza and Canyon View Information Plaza, but these tend to fill early.

Supai

- From Flagstaff, drive 70 miles west on I-40, then exit onto Arizona 66 at Seligman. Drive 30 miles west, and then turn right on Supai Highway. Continue 58 miles to the Hualapai Hilltop Trailhead at the end of the road. The Hualapai Trail is 8 miles to Supai Village.
- From Kingman, drive 58 miles east on Arizona 66 (Andy Devine Avenue), and then turn left on Supai Highway. Continue 58 miles to the Hualapai Hilltop Trailhead at the end of the road. The Hualapai Trail is 8 miles to Supai Village.

Grand Canyon West

From Kingman, drive 44 miles north on Stockton Hill Road, and then turn right and drive 6.4 miles on Pierce Ferry Road. Turn right on Diamond Bar Road, and drive 16.6 miles. Turn left on Buck and Doe Road, and drive 4.5 miles to Grand Canyon West Airport. Portions of this road are dirt.

North Rim

Note: The North Rim is closed from mid-October through mid-May.

- From Flagstaff, drive 109 miles north on US 89. Turn left on US 89A, and drive 55 miles north to Jacob Lake. (There is a Forest Service Visitor Center at Jacob Lake.) Turn left on Arizona 67, and drive 43 miles, passing the North Entrance Station, to North Rim Village.

- From Kanab, Utah, drive 37 miles south on US 89A to Jacob Lake. (There is a Forest Service Visitor Center at Jacob Lake.) Turn right on Arizona 67, and drive 43 miles, passing the North Entrance Station, to North Rim Village.

Toroweap

From Kanab, Utah, drive 7 miles south on US 89A. Turn right on Arizona 389. Drive 8.3 miles west, and then turn right on dirt County Road 109 (Mount Trumbull Road). After 37 miles, stay left on CR 5. Drive 6 miles, and then stay left on CR 115. Continue 14 miles, passing the Toroweap Ranger Station, to Toroweap Overlook and Campground.

Grand Canyon-Parashant National Monument

The national monument is approximately 30 miles southwest of St. George, Utah. The main access is from St. George, south on River Road 8 miles to the Utah/Arizona border. From here, several dirt roads provide access to points within the monument. All of the roads on the national monument are dirt and are impassable in wet weather. There are no services or facilities in the national monument, so visitors must be prepared for desert back road driving and camping.

National Park Entrance Fees

National Park entrance permits and passes cover entrance fees to the national park only and do not cover campground fees. You can purchase an entrance permit, valid for seven days, or several different passes, which are valid for one year or more. Permits and passes can be obtained at the park entrance stations, at ranger stations and visitor centers in the park, and at businesses outside the park.

Other Fees

Some Grand Canyon destinations outside the national park and monument charge fees which are not covered by National Park passes. These destinations include Supai on the Havasupai Indian Reservation and Grand Canyon West on the Hualapai Indian Reservation. See Supai and Grand Canyon West for more information.

Entry Permits and Passes

- Vehicle Permit: $25, admits one private vehicle and all its passengers

- Individual Permit: $12, admits one person, arriving on foot, bicycle, or motorcycle

- Grand Canyon National Park Annual Pass: $50, good for one year at Grand Canyon National Park

- America the Beautiful Pass: $80, good for one year at all national parks and other federal recreation sites that charge entrance fees

- America the Beautiful Senior Pass: $10, a lifetime pass to all federal lands charging an entrance fee, including national parks. Available to U.S. citizens or permanent residents age 62 and over.

- America the Beautiful Access Pass: Free, a lifetime pass to all federal lands charging an entrance fee, including national parks. Available to U.S. citizens or permanent residents with permanent disabilities.

- America the Beautiful Volunteer Pass: Free, valid for one year at all federal lands charging an entrance fee, including national parks. Available to volunteers who have done 500 hours of volunteer service on an annual basis.

For more details on entrance fees and passes, see the park website: www.nps.gov/grca/planyourvisit/entrance-fees.htm

Scenic Drives

There are two roads at the South Rim and one on the North Rim that offer excellent scenic drives.

Hermit Road closely follows the rim west of Grand Canyon Village past several spectacular viewpoints. Access is by free shuttle bus most of the year. The Hermit Shuttle stops at all of the major viewpoints on the outbound trip, so you can get off at any viewpoint, spend as long as you like, and catch the next shuttle. You can also walk the Rim Trail between viewpoints.

Desert View Drive runs along the rim east of Grand Canyon Village and passes several viewpoints with a great variety of views of the eastern Grand Canyon. There is no shuttle service.

On the North Rim, Cape Royal Road winds through the beautiful alpine forest on the Kaibab Plateau passing several viewpoints before ending at one of the finest viewpoints on either rim of the Grand Canyon.

The scenic drives are described in the South Rim and North Rim chapters:

- Hermit Road

- Desert View Drive

- Cape Royal Road

Lodging and Restaurants

We have fallen heirs to the most glorious heritage a people ever received, and each one must do his part if we wish to show that the nation is worthy of its good fortune. - *Theodore Roosevelt*

El Tovar Hotel

The South Rim has most of the lodging and restaurants that are in or near the park. The North Rim has one lodge, Grand Canyon Lodge, within the park, and two outside the park on AZ 67- Jacob Lake Inn and Kaibab Lodge. All of the North Rim lodges have restaurants. There is also a resort at the bottom of the canyon along the Kaibab Trail, Phantom Ranch, which can be accessed by hiking the trail or by mule trip.

Advance Reservations Recommended

Rooms are scarce during the busy period from March through mid-November, so be sure to make advance reservations.

Lodging Within the Park

South Rim and Phantom Ranch

- Xanterra operates the South Rim lodges and Phantom Ranch- for reservations, call 888-297-2727 or 303-297-2757. For same day reservations, call 928-638-9810. Xanterra website: www.grandcanyonlodges.com

9

- El Tovar Hotel: One of the classic national park lodges and a National Historic Landmark, El Tovar opened in 1905 and was renovated in 2005. The hotel features a dining room that is open all day. It is located on the South Rim in Grand Canyon Village.

- Bright Angel Lodge was designed by famed Southwestern architect Mary Jane Colter in 1935 as a rustic lodge and is also a National Historic Landmark. It is located on the South Rim at the west end of Grand Canyon Village. There are two restaurants.

- Kachina Lodge is a modern lodge located on the South Rim between Bright Angel Lodge and El Tovar. Some rooms have partial Canyon views. It is a short walk to the restaurants at El Tovar and Bright Angel Lodge.

- Thunderbird Lodge is another modern lodge on the rim between El Tovar and Bright Angel Lodge. As with Kachina Lodge, some rooms have partial Canyon views. It is a short walk to the restaurants at El Tovar and Bright Angel Lodge.

- Maswik Lodge is located at the southwest corner of Grand Canyon Village, about 1/4 mile from the South Rim. It is a motel-style lodge with a cafeteria and sports bar. Rustic cabins are available during the summer.

- Yavapai Lodge is the largest lodge on the South Rim within the park, and is located near Market Plaza in Grand Canyon Village, about 1/2 mile from the South Rim. There is a cafe which is open all day, and the park Visitor Center is close by at Canyon View Information Plaza. Market Plaza has a grocery store, bank, and post office.

- Phantom Ranch is a unique lodge designed by Mary Jane Colter and is located along Bright Angel Creek and the North Kaibab Trail, just north of the Colorado River. It is the only lodge located at the bottom of the canyon. Phantom Ranch can only be reached by foot, mule, or via a Colorado River trip. Overnight mule trips include a stay at Phantom Ranch- all others must make reservations for lodging and meals in advance. The canteen serves snacks and beverages.

North Rim

- Grand Canyon Lodge is the only lodge on the North Rim within the park, and it is operated by Forever Resorts. It is located near Bright Angel Point on the North Rim. A National Historic Landmark, Grand Canyon Lodge is unique among national park lodges in that the main building doesn't have guest rooms. Instead, as you enter, you get your first glimpse of the Grand Canyon through the sweeping view windows of the veranda. Separate cabins provide the accommodations, and there is a dining room off the veranda. To make reservations, call 877-386-4383 or 480-337-1320. Forever Resorts Website: http://foreverlodging.com/lodging.cfm?PropertyKey=181

Lodging Outside the Park

South Rim

There are a large number of motels and hotels located in Tusayan, about 10 miles south of the South Rim just outside the park, and in the cities of Williams and Flagstaff along I-40. For central lodging reservations, call 800-916-8530, or visit the Grand Canyon Hotels and Lodges website: www.grandcanyon.com/hotels.html

North Rim

There are two lodges on the Kaibab Plateau north of the North Rim along AZ 67, the access highway.

- Jacob Lake Inn is located at the junction of US 89A and AZ 67 about 43 miles north of the North Rim. The inn was built in 1923 and is nestled in the towering pines of the Kaibab National Forest. Jacob Lake Inn has a cafe featuring locally baked goods, as well as a gift shop with local native arts and crafts, and a gas station. The Kaibab National Forest Visitor Center is just south of the inn. For reservations, call 928-643-7232, or visit the Jacob Lake Inn website: www.jacoblake.com

- Kaibab Lodge is located on the edge of DeMotte Park in the Kaibab National Forest, about 10 miles north of the North Rim along AZ 67. The lodge has a restaurant, and there is a gas station and general store across the highway. Kaibab Lodge is open from did–May through mid-October, and closed in the winter. For reservations, call 928-638-2389, or visit theKaibab Lodge website: www.kaibablodge.com

Restaurants and Dining

All of the lodges listed above have dining at the lodge or nearby. In addition, the towns of Tusayan, Williams, and Flagstaff, south of the South Rim, also have numerous cafes, restaurants, and fast food. In the area of the North Rim, the nearest towns with restaurants and fast food are Fredonia on US 89A and Page on US 89, and Kanab, Utah, on US 89. See the Grand Canyon Region Map on page 3.

Camping

Westerners live outdoors more than people elsewhere because outdoors is mainly what they've got. -Wallace Stegner

Back country camping in the Grand Canyon

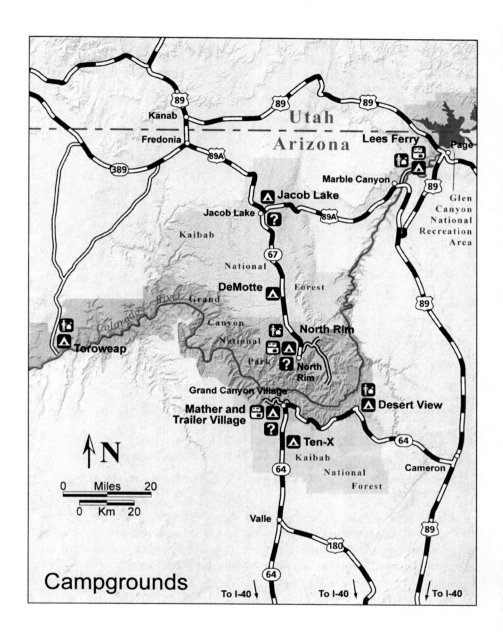

Campgrounds

Both Grand Canyon National Park and the surrounding Kaibab National Forest have developed vehicle campgrounds. There are no campgrounds in Grand Canyon-Parashant National Monument or the Havasupai or Hualapai reservations. All of the campgrounds except for Toroweap charge a nightly fee.

Backcountry Camping

Except for those holding a backcountry camping permit, camping is limited to developed campgrounds within the national park. Camping at undeveloped sites is allowed on the Kaibab National Forest.

South Rim

Mather Campground

Location: Grand Canyon Village near Market Plaza

Season: All year

Units: 315

Tents: Yes

RVs and Trailers: Up to 30 feet

Dump Station: Yes, except in winter

Hookups: No

Water: Yes

Showers: Yes, at Market Plaza

Self-Serve Laundry: Yes, at Market Plaza

Handicap-Accessible: Yes

Management: Grand Canyon National Park, www.nps.gov/grca

Reservations: National Recreation Reservation Service, www.recreation.gov, 877-444-6777

Mather Campground is the largest in the Grand Canyon area and the only one open all year. Pets are allowed but must be leashed at all times and must not be left unattended. Wood gathering is not permitted, but wood is available at the general store in Market Plaza. Reservations are strongly recommended during the busy season from March through October.

Trailer Village

Location: Grand Canyon Village near Market Plaza

Season: All year

Units: 78

Tents: No

RVs and Trailers: Yes

Dump Station: Yes, except in winter

Hookups: Yes, all sites

Water: Yes

Showers: Yes, at Market Plaza

Self-Serve Laundry: Yes, at Market Plaza

Handicap-Accessible: Yes

Management: Grand Canyon National Park, www.nps.gov/grca

Reservations: 888-297-2757 or 928-638-2631

Trailer Village is located next to Mather Campground in Grand Canyon Village.

Desert View Campground

Location: Desert View

Season: May to mid-October

Units: 50

Tents: Yes

RVs and Trailers: Yes, up to 30 feet

Dump Station: No

Hookups: No

Water: Yes

Showers: No

Self-Serve Laundry: No

Handicap-Accessible: Yes

Management: Grand Canyon National Park, www.nps.gov/grca

Reservations: First-come, first-served

Located at Desert View at the east end of Desert View Drive, this campground can handle some RVs up to 30 feet but most sites are designed for smaller RVs, trailers, or tents. Pets are allowed but must be leashed at all times and cannot be left unattended.

Ten-X Campground

Location: Two miles south of Tusayan

Season: May to September

Units: 70

Tents: Yes

RVs and Trailers: Yes, up to 40 feet

Dump Station: No

Hookups: No

Water: Yes

Showers: No

Self-Serve Laundry: No

Handicap-Accessible: Yes

Management: Kaibab National Forest, www.fs.fed.us/r3/kai

Reservations: National Recreation Reservation Service, www.recreation.gov, 877-444-6777

This campground is two miles south of Tusayan on the east side of AZ 64. Firewood may be collected outside the campground. Two group campsites are available and must be reserved in advance.

Lees Ferry

Lees Ferry Campground

Location: Five miles from Marble Canyon at Lees Ferry

Season: All year

Units: 30

Tents: Yes

RVs and Trailers: Yes

Dump Station: Yes

Hookups: No

Water: Yes

Showers: No

Self-Serve Laundry: At Marble Canyon

Handicap-Accessible: Yes

Management: Glen Canyon National Recreation Area, www.nps.gov/glca

Reservations: First-come, first-served

This campground is located at the head of Marble Canyon at historic Lees Ferry, where most Grand Canyon river trips begin. Fishing is popular on the Colorado River, and a boat ramp is available. A general store and gas station are located five miles away at Marble Canyon.

North Rim

North Rim Campground

Location: North Rim Village

Season: Mid-May to mid-October

Units: 83

Tents: Yes

RVs and Trailers: Yes

Dump Station: Yes

Hookups: No

Water: Yes

Showers: At campground entrance

Self-Serve Laundry: At campground entrance

Handicap-Accessible: Yes

Management: Grand Canyon National Park, www.nps.gov/grca

Reservations: National Recreation Reservation Service, www.recreation.gov, 877-444-6777

North Rim Campground is located just north of the North Rim Village on the entrance road. Collection of firewood is not allowed, but wood may be purchased at the adjacent general store. Because sites fill up early, reservations are strongly recommended.

Toroweap Campground

Location: Toroweap Overlook

Season: All year, but access road may be impassable after a winter storm

Units: 9

Tents: Yes

RVs and Trailers: No

Dump Station: No

Hookups: No

Water: No

Showers: No

Self-Serve Laundry: No

Handicap-Accessible: No

Management: Grand Canyon National Park, www.nps.gov/grca

Reservations: First-come, first-served

This campground is located just north of Toroweap Overlook. There are 11 sites, available on a first-come, first-served basis. Water is not available. See the Toroweap chapter for more information on the area.

DeMotte Campground

Location: On AZ 67, 25 miles south of Jacob Lake

Season: Mid-May through October, depending on snowfall

Units: 38

Tents: Yes

RVs and Trailers: Yes

Dump Station: No

Hookups: No

Water: Yes

Showers: No

Self-Serve Laundry: No

Handicap-Accessible: Yes

Management: Kaibab National Forest, www.fs.fed.us/r3/kai

Reservations: First-come, first-served

DeMotte Campground is seven miles north of the North Entrance to Grand Canyon National Park, and is located on the edge of beautiful DeMotte Park. Nearby Kaibab Lodge has rooms and a restaurant, and there is a general store and service station across the highway.

Jacob Lake Campground

Location: Jacob Lake at the junction of US 89A and AZ 67

Season: Mid-May through October, depending on snowfall

Units: 51

Tents: Yes

RVs and Trailers: Yes

Dump Station: No

Hookups: No

Water: Yes

Showers: No

Self-Serve Laundry: No

Handicap-Accessible: Yes

Management: Kaibab National Forest, www.fs.fed.us/r3/kai

Reservations: First-come, first-served

This campground is located in the ponderosa pine forest across from Jacob Lake Lodge. The lodge has rooms, a restaurant, a general store, and a service station.

Hiking

You cannot see the Grand Canyon in one view, as if it were a changeless spectacle from which a curtain might be lifted, but to see it you have to toil from month to month through its labyrinths. It is a region more difficult to traverse than the Alps or the Himalayas, but if strength and courage are sufficient for the task by a year's toil a concept of sublimity can be obtained never again to be equaled on the hither side of Paradise. -Major John Wesley Powell

Hiker in the Grand Canyon

One of the best ways to experience the Grand Canyon is to take a walk. Whether it's a few minutes stroll along a paved rim trail, or a ten day trek through a remote corner of the canyon, a walk takes you away from the distractions of our civilization and lets you experience the natural quiet of the Grand Canyon.

Take It Easy

Whether or not you're an experienced hiker, take it easy until you get used to the Grand Canyon. High altitude, dry air, and summer heat can cause problems for anyone. Travel at the speed of the slowest member of your group, and stop often to enjoy the view.

The Ten Essentials

Hike Prepared! Remember that the temperature rises as you descend into the canyon, especially during the summer. Always be prepared for heat and sudden weather changes, injuries, and delays because of slow hikers. Carry these essentials on anything longer than a casual stroll:

- Plenty of water

- Extra food

- Sunglasses

- Sunscreen

- Map

- Compass

- Knife

- Lighter or fire starter

- Rain gear and extra clothes

- First aid kit

It is always a good idea to check the park's website for Trail and backcountry hiking conditions, closures, and updates: www.nps.gov/grca/planyourvisit/trail-closures.htm

Hiking Permits

A backcountry permit is required for all overnight or longer hikes anywhere in the park. Permits for popular areas can be difficult to obtain, so it is advisable to apply well in advance, and have alternate trip plans.

The permit system is complex- check the park website for details: www.nps.gov/grca/planyourvisit/backcountry-permit.htm

Permits are required for all access to the Hualapai Indian Reservation and the Havasupai Indian Reservation, including hiking, backpacking, and camping.

Permits are not required for day hikes in Grand Canyon National Park, or for day hikes, backpacking, or camping on the public lands surrounding the park, including the Kaibab National Forest and Grand Canyon-Parashant National Monument.

Day Hikes

South Rim

Rim Trail

The Rim Trail follows the South Rim for nearly 12 miles from Hermits Rest to Pipe Creek Vista. It is an excellent trail to start with as elevation changes are limited to 300

Rim Trail in winter

feet, and the Village, Hermit, and Kaibab Trail shuttles stop at all the major viewpoints along the trail. You can walk between shuttle stops and make the hike as long or short as you want. In addition, portions of the Rim Trail are paved and graded to be handicap-accessible.

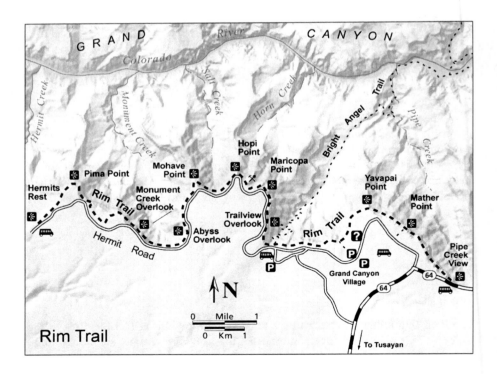

Upper South Kaibab Trail

A great day hike is from the South Kaibab Trailhead (accessible only via the Kaibab Shuttle) to Cedar Ridge, a distance of 1.5 miles one way. There are panoramic views of O'Neill Butte and the canyon as the trail comes out onto a ridge. Remember, the return hike is all uphill and much harder. There is no water along the trail. Do not attempt to hike to the river and back in one day!

O'Neill Butte on the South Kaibab Trail

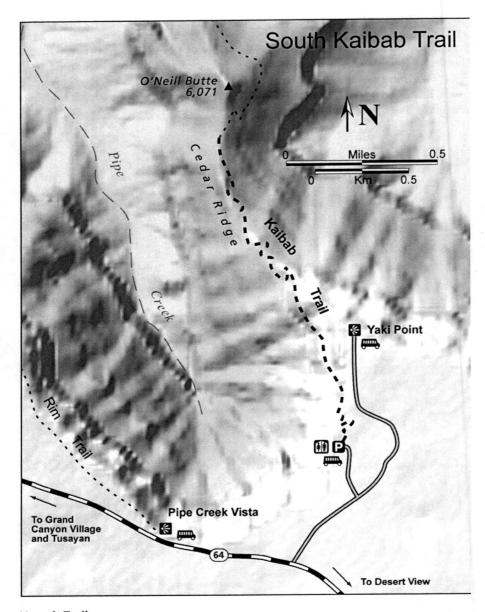

South Kaibab Trail

O'Neill Butte
6,071

N

Pipe

Cedar Ridge

Kaibab Trail

Creek

Yaki Point

Rim Trail

P

To Grand
Canyon Village
and Tusayan

Pipe Creek Vista

64

To Desert View

Hermit Trail

This unmaintained trail starts from Hermits Rest at the end of the Hermit Road. Good destinations are Santa Maria Spring, which is 2.5 miles each way, and Dripping Spring, which is 3.5 miles each way. Neither spring is reliable, so carry your own water. Both destinations offer excellent views of Hermit Canyon. Do not attempt to hike to the river and back in one day!

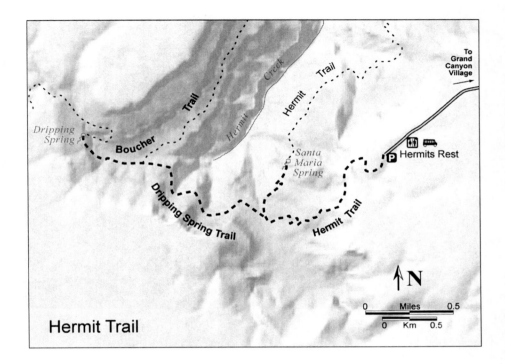

Hermit Trail

Grandview Trail

This trail starts from Grandview Point on Desert View Drive. Horseshoe Mesa, 3.0 miles each way, is a great destination. The Grandview Trail is unmaintained and is much rougher and slower going than the Kaibab or Bright Angel trails. You can easily spend a few hours exploring the historic mining district. Caution: Stay out of old mine shafts.

Hiking the Grandview Trail

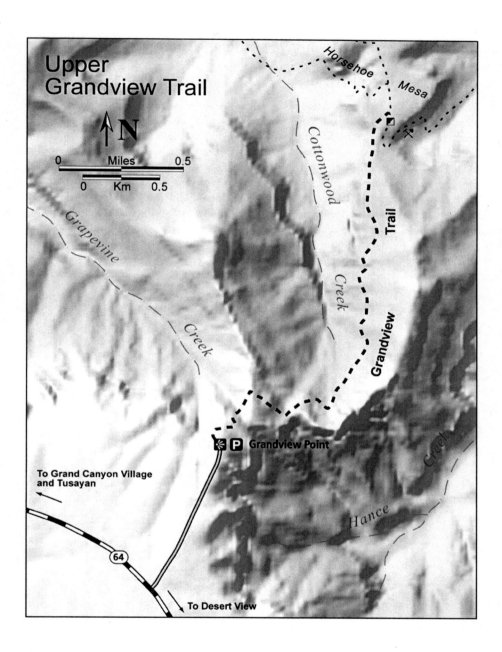

Upper Grandview Trail

N

0   Miles   0.5

0   Km   0.5

Horsehoe Mesa

Cottonwood Creek

Grandview Trail

Grapevine Creek

Grandview Point

To Grand Canyon Village and Tusayan

Hance Creek

64

To Desert View

Kaibab National Forest- Tusayan Ranger District

Arizona Trail- Coconino Rim

A section of the 800-mile Arizona Trail follows the Coconino Rim southeast from Grandview Fire Lookout on the Tusayan District of the Kaibab National Forest. To reach this trailhead, drive east on Desert View Drive to the Grandview Point junction. Continue 2.0 miles east on Desert Drive, and then turn right onto the Coconino Rim Road. Drive this dirt road 1.2 miles. You'll see the Arizona Trail trailhead on the left, just after crossing the park boundary into the national forest.

Follow the Arizona Trail east from the trailhead. The trail wanders through the pleasant mixed forest of ponderosa pine, pinyon pine, and juniper as it loosely follows the Coconino Rim. A good destination for a day hike is a point 3.1 miles, one-way, from the trailhead, where the Arizona Trail reaches a sharply-defined, eastward-facing section of the Coconino Rim with excellent views.

For more information on the Arizona Trail, see the Arizona Trail Association website: www.aztrail.org.

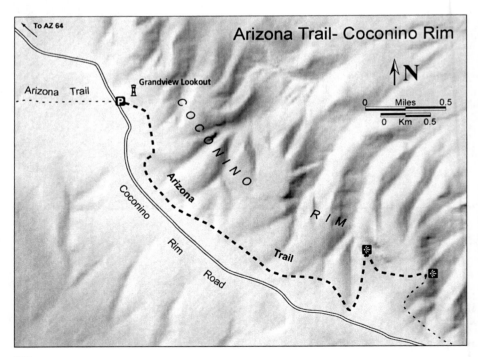

North Rim

Transept Trail

The Transept Trail follows the rim of Transept Canyon from Grand Canyon Lodge to North Rim Campground, a distance of 1.4 miles one-way. The trail is nearly level.

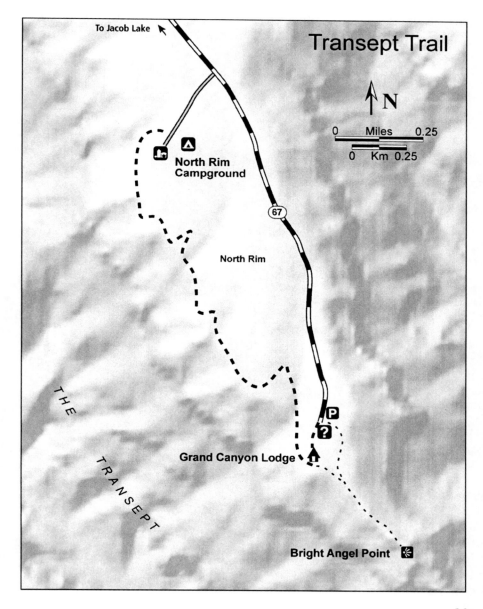

Widforss Trail

The Widforss Trail starts from a trailhead across the road from the North Kaibab Trailhead, and winds 4.4 miles along the west rim of the Transept to a point on the North Rim overlooking Widforss Point.

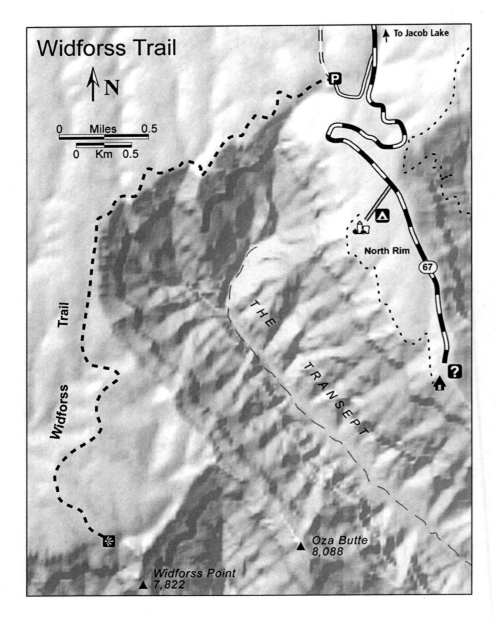

Ken Patrick Trail

This trail connects Point Imperial with the North Kaibab Trailhead, a distance of 10 miles. If you plan to hike the entire trail, it is best to hike it one way with a car shuttle. The trail skirts the rim after leaving Point Imperial, then crosses the Point Imperial Road and wanders through the forest to the North Kaibab Trailhead.

Uncle Jim Trail

This 2.5-mile trail starts at the North Kaibab Trailhead and traverses the forest to a viewpoint overlooking Roaring Springs Canyon and the Kaibab Trail.

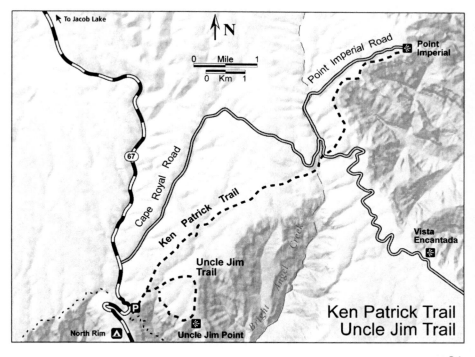

Cape Final Trail

This trail starts from the Cape Final Trailhead along the Cape Royal Road and follows an old fire road 2.0 miles through the rim forest to Cape Final, a major promontory with excellent views of the eastern Grand Canyon.

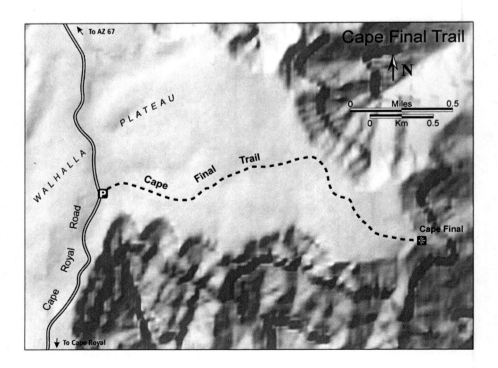

North Kaibab Trail

The park's trans-canyon trail, the North Kaibab Trail starts from the North Kaibab Trailhead just north of the village, descends into Roaring Springs Canyon, and then follows Bright Angel Creek to Phantom Ranch and the Colorado River, a distance of 14 miles one-way and a descent of 5,950 feet. Do not attempt to hike to the river and back in one day! A day hike to Supai Tunnel and back is a good short day hike. This

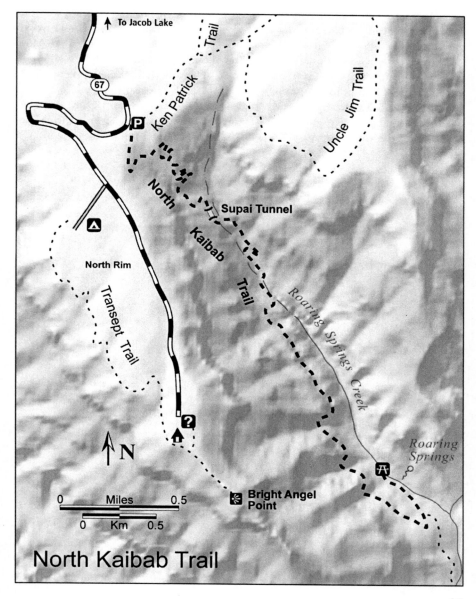

North Kaibab Trail

hike is 2.0 miles each way and a descent of 1,400 feet. For an all day hike, you can hike down to Roaring Springs and back, which is 4.7 miles each way and a descent of 3,050 feet.

Kaibab National Forest- North Kaibab Ranger District

Arizona Trail- North Canyon Loop

This strenuous 3.7-mile loop hike uses sections of both the North Canyon and Arizona trails to loop down into the head of North Canyon, past a spring, and then back along the rim of North Canyon. To reach the trailhead, start from Jacob Lake at the junction of US 89A and AZ 67, and drive 26 miles south on AZ 67 to DeMotte Park. Turn left on Forest Road 611 and follow the signs four miles to East Rim View.

Descend into North Canyon via the North Canyon Trail, which descends 1,400 feet in about 1.4 miles to the bottom of the canyon. Then turn right, and follow the trail up the bed of the canyon. As the trail nears the head of North Canyon, it veers right and climbs steeply up the west fork, passing North Canyon Spring, and continues to the rim, a distance of 1.6 miles. Turn right and follow the Arizona Trail north 1.7 miles to East Rim View.

For an alternative, easier hike, follow the Arizona Trail south along the rim of North Canyon for 1.7 miles, one way, and then return the way you came.

For more information on the Arizona Trail, see the Arizona Trail Association website: www.aztrail.org.

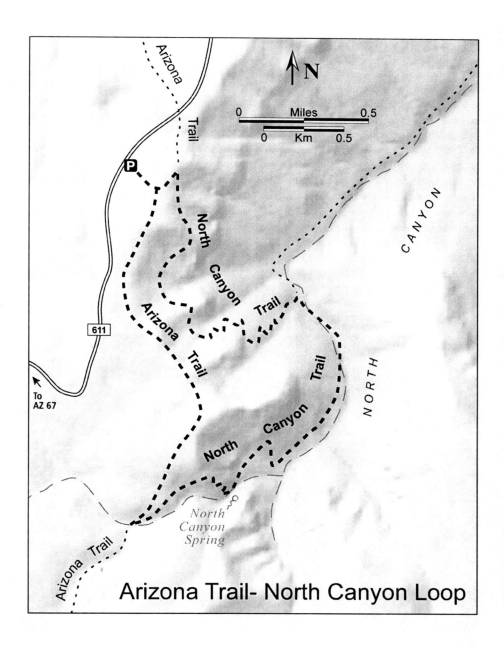

Arizona Trail- North Canyon Loop

Backpack Trips

Backpacking in the Grand Canyon is extremely rewarding for those who are both experienced and equipped. Even if you are an experienced mountain backpacker, the Grand Canyon is different. It is desert backpacking, where the trip must be planned around the available water sources. During the summer, hikers may need as much as two gallons of water per person per day.

Trails and routes in the canyon are defined by the persistent horizontal cliff bands, and even though you may be able to see a spring or stream from above, you may not be able to reach it. For its size, Grand Canyon has very few trails. Only the Kaibab and Bright Angel Trails are maintained- the remaining dozen are leftover prospector trails, maintained primarily by use. These trails are generally unsigned and may fade out without warning, or be confused by multiple routes.

Many backpack trips in the Grand Canyon require difficult cross-country hiking. Unless a member of your party is an experienced Grand Canyon backpacker, spend some time hiking the backcountry trails and learning how to route find in the canyon before attempting any cross-country hike.

Trails in the Canyon often follow narrow ledges between tall cliffs

Seasons

The best seasons for backpacking in the Grand Canyon are spring and fall, when the canyon temperatures are moderate. Winter can be a good season as well, though the top several thousand feet of the trails may be snow-covered.

36

Avoid hiking during the summer heat, from May through September! Temperatures reach 110 degrees F in the lower parts of the canyon and any mistakes you make, especially with regard to water, quickly become fatal.

Refer to www.GrandCanyonGuide.net for a list of hiking guide books and maps: www.GrandCanyonGuide.net/books/books.html.

South Rim

Kaibab-Bright Angel Loop

The classic first-time backpack trip in the Canyon, this loop is often done as an overnighter, but there's so much to explore that you could easily use up five days. The loop starts from the Kaibab Trailhead and returns to the Bright Angel Trailhead. Since both of these South Rim trailheads are served by free year-round shuttle buses, leave your car at the Backcountry Office.

The South Kaibab Trail is the best way to start the loop, because the trail spends a lot of time on ridges and offers great views during the steady descent. Allow half a day for the hike to Phantom Ranch and Bright Angel Campground.

You can use Bright Angel Campground (or Phantom Ranch, if you make reservations) as a base for exploration up the North Kaibab Trail to Ribbon Falls and Phantom Canyon's impressive gorge. Because of flash flood danger, stay out of Phantom Canyon during stormy weather. Make time for a side hike up the Clear

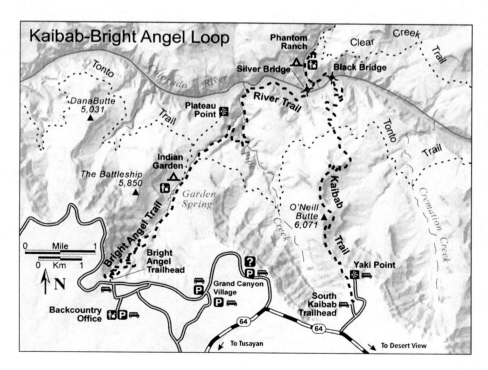

37

Below The Tipoff on the South Kaibab Trail

Creek Trail to the Tonto Plateau for stunning views of Granite Gorge.

Return to the South Rim via the Silver Bridge, River Trail, and Bright Angel Trail. Though longer than the South Kaibab Trail, this route has gentler grades and a variety of scenery. You could also camp at Indian Gardens, and spend some time doing a side hike out to Plateau Point. Other options for exploration include the Tonto Trail to the east and to the west.

Boucher-Hermit Loop

This great loop hike starts from Hermits Rest at the end of the Hermit Road. Use the free Hermit Shuttle to reach the trailhead, except during winter when the shuttle is not running. (There is trailhead parking down a short gravel road beyond the main parking lot.) This loop makes a nice three day trip, though you could easily expand it to four or five days.

Follow the Hermit Trail down through impressive construction in the Coconino Sandstone past the junction with the Waldron Trail. At the second junction, turn left onto the Dripping Spring Trail, and follow this trail across the top of the Supai Group cliffs at the head of Hermit Canyon to the Boucher Trail. Turn right, and follow the Boucher Trail along the top of the Supai, down into the head of White Creek, through the saddle next to White Butte, and eventually down to the Tonto Trail. Take the Tonto Trail a short distance west into Boucher Creek. The ruins of the Hermit's (Louis Boucher) mine and cabin are still present near the creek, which has permanent water- if not at the trail crossing, then a short distance downstream. The cross-country hike down Boucher Creek to the river is easy, and only takes a few hours round-trip.

Along the Hermit Trail

The hike continues east on the Tonto Trail, which winds around Travertine Canyon before reaching Hermit Creek and its permanent water. Here, you can hike cross-country down Hermit Creek to the Colorado River to catch a view of the huge waves of Hermit Rapid, and also spend some time exploring the remains of Hermit Camp. This tourist camp was the main resort below the rim until the opening of Phantom Ranch on the Kaibab Trail. It was supplied by a 4,000-foot aerial tramway from Pima Point on the South Rim.

Hike east on the Tonto Trail to reach the junction with the Hermit Trail, your trail out of the Canyon. After a long climb up the Tonto slopes, a tight series of switchbacks ascend the Redwall Limestone at Cathedral Stairs. The Hermit Trail then climbs across the Supai Group slopes, switchbacking up through breaks in the cliff bands, and eventually reaches the old resthouse and watering trough at Santa Maria Spring (the spring is seasonal and not reliable.) After climbing through the Esplanade Sandstone at the top of the Supai Group, the Hermit Trail passes the junctions with the Dripping Spring and Waldron trails, and continues to the rim at Hermits Rest.

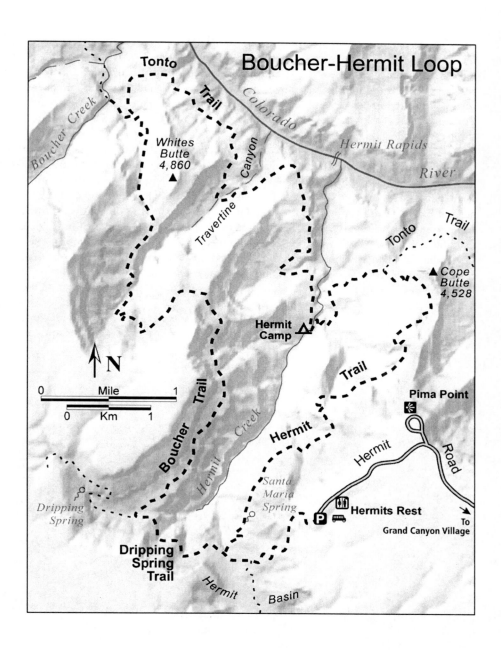

Boucher-Hermit Loop

Tonto
Trail

Whites
Butte
4,860

Boucher Creek

Colorado

Hermit Rapids

River

Travertine Canyon

Tonto

Trail

Cope
Butte
4,528

**Hermit
Camp**

Trail

Pima Point

N

Boucher Trail

Hermit Creek

Hermit

Hermit

Road

0   Mile   1
0   Km   1

Santa
Maria
Spring

P

Hermits Rest

To
Grand Canyon Village

Dripping
Spring

**Dripping
Spring
Trail**

Hermit

Basin

Tanner-Grandview

This gorgeous hike in the eastern Grand Canyon takes you through a startling change in the geology at the floor of the canyon, where the open shale hills of the Tanner area give way to the somber Granite Gorge. The hike starts at the Tanner Trailhead at Lipan Point and ends at the Grandview Trailhead at Grandview Point, so you'll need to do a short car shuttle along Desert View Drive.

The Tanner Trail starts a few yards down the access road below the Lipan Point parking area. The unmaintained trail descends rapidly through the rim formations via a series of short switchbacks, then levels out and crosses the saddle at the head of Seventyfive Mile Canyon. Descending gradually through the Supai Group as it swings around Escalante and Cardenas buttes, the Tanner Trail reaches the rim of the Redwall Limestone above Tanner Canyon. A few broad switchbacks lead onto the Tonto slope, and the trail winds past some impressive slump blocks of Tapeats Sandstone before descending along a ridge in the shales of the Grand Canyon Supergroup. The trail reaches the Colorado River at the mouth of Tanner Canyon. Most hikers will spend half a day descending the Tanner Trail, so you may want to continue downriver before camping.

The hike continues downriver to the mouth of Cardenas Creek along an informal trail. There are campsites near the river and also upstream in a short narrows in Cardenas Creek.

Tanner Trail at the Colorado River

Continue the hike by following the cairned route and informal trail up Cardenas Creek and then onto the ridge above Unkar Rapid. The trail climbs the ridge to the south until just below the Tapeats Sandstone cliff, then turns west and contours around the end of the fin of Tapeats Sandstone. South of the fin, the route drops into Escalante Creek and follows the bed to the river, except for a couple of places where the trail leaves the bed to bypass dry waterfalls.

At the river, the trail follows the left bank downriver for a few yards before being forced to follow a rising ramp in the Shinumo Quartzite to avoid the cliffs along the river's edge. The trail follows the ramp around into Seventyfive Mile Canyon and upstream above an impressive lower gorge in the quartzite before finding a break. Descend to the bed of Seventyfive Mile Canyon when you can and then follow the bed downstream back to the Colorado River.

The trail stays at rivers edge for nearly a mile to the mouth of Papago Creek. Most hikers will take a day to travel the informal trail from Tanner Canyon or Cardenas Creek to Papago Creek, and the camping is better here than along the next stretch.

Cliffs block the route downriver from Papago Creek. To continue down river, walk a few yards up Papago Creek and follow a cairned route up ledges and to the right to a break where you can descend back to river level. It's now a easy hike downriver to the mouth of Red Canyon.

The Red Canyon Trail climbs up Red Canyon to the South Rim, but a better hike is to follow the Tonto Trail, which also starts at the mouth of Red Canyon. The Tonto Trail crosses a sand flat above Hance Rapid and then climbs around into Mineral Canyon. After crossing Mineral Canyon, the Tonto Trail climbs to reach the beginnings of the Tonto Platform north of Coronado Butte. The trail then meanders south along the Tonto Platform to cross Hance Creek. If Hance Creek is dry at the trail crossing, you can usually find water a short distance downstream. You can camp here, or shorten the climb out of the Canyon by ascending the east side Grandview Trail to the backcountry campsite on Horseshoe Mesa. Horseshoe Mesa is dry, so you will have to carry water for a dry camp.

Leaving the Tonto Trail on the west side of Hance Creek, the east side Grandview Trail climbs past a spur trail to Miners Spring (located on the north side of the unnamed canyon, at the base of the Redwall Limestone), passes shafts from the Last Chance Mine, and climbs to the Redwall Limestone rim on the east side of Horseshoe Mesa. The old mine cookshack and the backcountry campground are north of this trail junction. The upper Grandview Trail climbs south up the slopes of the Supai Group and then works its way through the Coconino Sandstone cliffs via some serious trail construction, finally ending at Grandview Point.

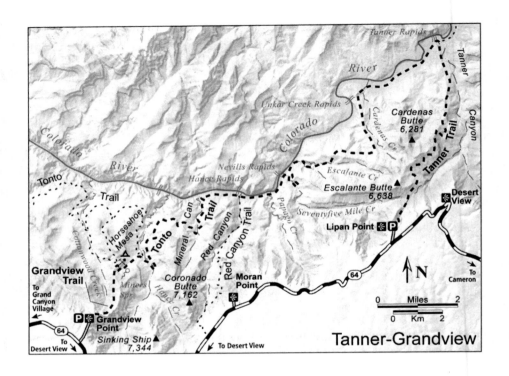

Sunset on Angels Gate

North Rim

North Kaibab Trail

While a lot of backpackers focus on using the trans-canyon Kaibab Trail to hike rim to rim, there's a lot to do along the North Kaibab Trail itself. Using the two campgrounds, Cottonwood Camp and Bright Angel Campground, as bases, you can explore such enticing places as upper Bright Angel Canyon (the route of the original North Kaibab Trail), The Transept, Ribbon Falls, Phantom Canyon, and the Clear Creek Trail. A nice overnight hike from the North Kaibab Trailhead is to Cottonwood Camp and back, but you could easily spend a week in the area.

Nankoweap Trail

This long, rough trail is a challenge to most hikers, but it leads into the beautiful Nankoweap Creek area with its permanent stream and easy access to the river. There are two trailheads for the Nankoweap Trail; most hikers use the Saddle Mountain Trailhead. To reach this trailhead, turn south on Buffalo Ranch Road about a mile east of the point where US 89A climbs onto the Kaibab Plateau. This graded road is passable to most vehicles, except after a major storm. It's 27.4 miles south to the signed trailhead for the Saddle Mountain and Nankoweap trails.

Follow the Saddle Mountain Trail down into Saddle Canyon, where you'll come to a junction and stay right on the Nankoweap Trail. This trail continues up Saddle Canyon and eventually climbs up a ridge through ponderosa pine forest to reach a large saddle just west of Saddle Mountain. (The original, seldom-used upper Nankoweap Trail descends from the North Rim north of Point Imperial, and comes in from the right just above this saddle). The Nankoweap Trail descends into the Grand Canyon via a series of short switchbacks but soon levels out and follows a terrace at the base of the Esplanade Sandstone (the uppermost cliff in the Supai Group.) It stays at this level, descending slowly with the tilt in the rock strata, all the way to Tilted Mesa. There is one tricky place where the original trail construction has fallen away and the hiker-maintained trail crosses a short but steep slope above a cliff. This spot is usually no trouble when the trail is dry, but can be a problem when the trail is muddy.

Just above Tilted Mesa, the Nankoweap Trail descends a ridge through the remainder of the Supai Group, then turns right and switchbacks down a broad slope through the Redwall Limestone. The trail thens heads generally southeast and comes out on the Tonto slope south of Tilted Mesa. It makes the final descent to Nankoweap Creek at the 3400-foot elevation contour. There are several spacious campsites here that you can use as a base for exploring Nankoweap Creek as well as south along the Horsethief Route. You can also follow Nankoweap Creek downstream to the Colorado River.

Hiker on the North Kaibab Trail

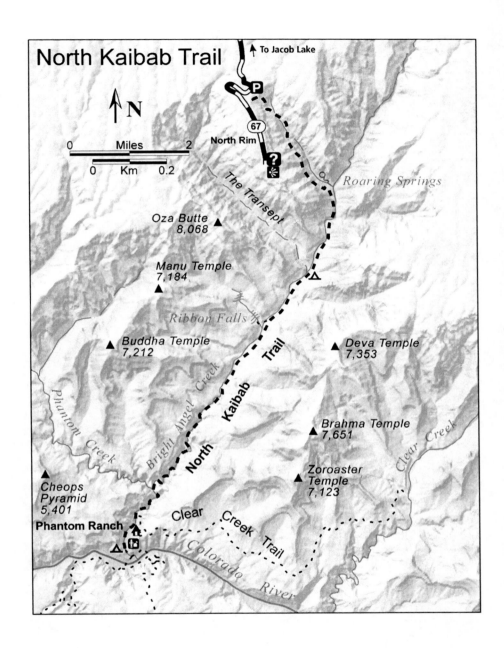

North Kaibab Trail

↑ To Jacob Lake

↑ N

P

67

North Rim

?

The Transept

Roaring Springs

Oza Butte
8,068 ▲

Manu Temple
7,184
▲

Ribbon Falls

Buddha Temple
7,212 ▲

Bright Angel Creek

North Kaibab Trail

Deva Temple
7,353 ▲

Brahma Temple
▲ 7,651

Phantom Creek

Clear Creek

Zoroaster
▲ Temple
7,123

Cheops
Pyramid
5,401 ▲

Phantom Ranch

Clear Creek Trail

△ 🏠

Colorado River

Scale:
0 — Miles — 2
0 — Km — 0.2

47

Picking up water from Nankoweap Creek

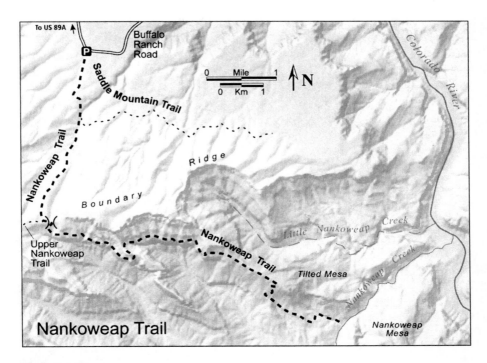

Nankoweap Trail

Map labels: To US 89A, Buffalo Ranch Road, Saddle Mountain Trail, Nankoweap Trail, Ridge, Boundary, Upper Nankoweap Trail, Nankoweap Trail, Little Nankoweap Creek, Nankoweap Creek, Tilted Mesa, Nankoweap Mesa, Colorado River, 0 Mile 1, 0 Km 1, N

Thunder River

By far the most popular of the North Rim's non-maintained trails, the Thunder River Trail takes you into an area with interesting geology, the world's shortest river, and aptly-named Thunder Spring, which roars out of a cave in the Redwall Limestone. You can do this as an overnight hike, but most backpackers like to take longer because of the long drive to the trailhead. There are plenty of side hikes that you can do from the Thunder River area.

Fall is the best season for a hike to Thunder River. Summer is too hot, and the access road is often impassable during the winter and spring.

Most hikers use the shorter Bill Hall Trail from Monument Point rather than the original trailhead from Indian Hollow. To reach the Bill Hall Trailhead from Jacob Lake on US 89A, drive south on AZ 67 0.4 miles, and then turn right onto Forest Road 461. Drive 5.2 miles, and then turn right onto FR 462. Continue 3.3 miles, and then turn left onto FR 422. Drive 11.4 miles, and then turn right onto FR 425. Drive 10.3 miles, and then bear right onto FR 292, which is the main road. Continue 2.9 miles as the road becomes FR 292A and ends at the Bill Hall Trailhead.

The Bill Hall Trail (named after a ranger who died in an accident) heads west along the rim to Monument Point, then descends steeply off the rim south of the point. It then heads north along the Toroweap Formation terraces to a break in the Coconino Sandstone, where it descends abruptly to the west to meet the Thunder River Trail on the broad terrace of the Esplanade. Turn left at this junction and follow the Thunder River Trail as the trail works it way south around drainages west of Bridgers Knoll. The trail then turns west and descends to a saddle. Turning south, the Thunder River

Hiker in Tapeats Creek

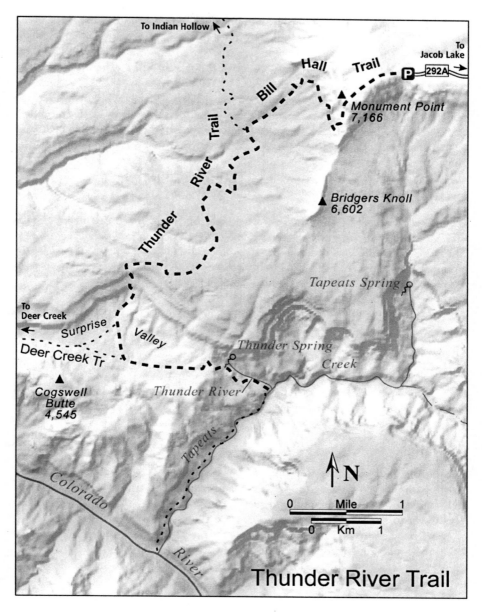

To Indian Hollow ↖ ·
To Jacob Lake
Hall   Trail
P ──[292A]→
Bill
▲
Monument Point
7,166
River   Trail
▲ *Bridgers Knoll*
6,602
Thunder
Tapeats Spring ♀
To
Deer Creek
←
Surprise   Valley
Thunder Spring
Creek
Deer Creek Tr
♀
▲
Cogswell
Butte
4,545
Thunder River
Tapeats
↑ **N**
Colorado
0   Mile   1
0   Km   1
River

Thunder River Trail

Trail descends the Redwall Limestone in a series of short, steep switchbacks, finally coming out onto gentler terrain in Surprise Valley. Stay left at two junctions with the trails to Deer Creek.

Surprise Valley is the top of a huge slump block, where a massive section of Redwall Limestone slid down and tilted as it dropped. Across the valley, the summit of Cogswell Butte consists of layers of Supai Group rocks on top of the Redwall slump block.

Continue east on the Thunder River Trail, which climbs a bit to reach the east rim of Surprise Valley. Here you are suddenly greeted with the roar of Thunder Spring bursting out of its Redwall Limestone cave to form Thunder River. The trail continues a steep descent alongside Thunder River past small campsites, and ends where Thunder River meets Tapeats Creek.

You can explore cross-country upstream along Tapeats Creek, where you'll have to wade through a short narrows in the Tapeats Sandstone. A well-worn river-runner's trail leads down Tapeats Creek to the Colorado River. Another possible side hike starts at the junction with the Deer Creek Trail in Surprise Valley, and follows the Deer Creek Trail to Deer Valley.

Guided Hikes

If you don't feel up to organizing your own hike, join a ranger-led day hike. For hikes with an educational emphasis, consider joining a trip lead by the Grand Canyon Field Institute. And finally, you can go with a commercial guide service authorized by the National Park Service. For more information, see the park's Guided Hikes page, www.nps.gov/grca/planyourvisit/guided-hikes.htm .

Cross-Country Skiing and Snowshoeing

South Rim

From December through March, there is often enough snow on the South Rim to cross-country ski and snowshoe. The Rim Trail from Yavapai Point to Pipe Creek Vista is especially scenic. The Greenway Trail through Grand Canyon Village is another great ski and snowshoe route.

North Rim

The North Rim offers a classic multi-day backcountry ski trip from Jacob Lake to North Rim Village following the snowed-over highway. This trip is 43 miles each way and should be attempted only by experienced backcountry skiers. A backcountry permit is required to enter the park.

Day cross-country ski or snowshoe trips on the Kaibab Plateau can be made off US 89A by following national forest roads.

Cross-country skiing along the Rim Trail

For Kids and Families

I am glad I shall never be young without wild country to be young in. Of what avail are 40 freedoms without a blank spot on the map? -Aldo Leopold

People at Mather Point

Family activities at Grand Canyon include ranger-led talks and hikes, the WebRanger program, and the Junior Ranger program.

The Rim Trail is for Families

Starting from Pipe Creek Vista just east of Grand Canyon Village and continuing to Hermits Rest at the west end of Hermit Road, the Rim Trail winds along the South Rim past several major viewpoints.

The Village, Kaibab and Hermit shuttles, which are free, stop at most of the viewpoints along the Rim Trail, so you can walk any portion of the trail one-way, then ride the shuttle between viewpoints, or back to your starting place.

Be a WebRanger!

If you have access to the Internet, you can become a National Park WebRanger, even if you're not at the Grand Canyon: www.webrangers.us. You can play more than 50 games, learn about the national parks, and share park stories and pictures with other WebRangers around the world.

Junior Ranger Programs

For a current list of all ranger programs, see the Ranger Program Schedule: www.nps.gov/grca/parknews/

Junior Rangers have fun learning about the Grand Canyon and the national park and represent the park to their friends and families. There are five ways you can become a Junior Ranger of Grand Canyon National Park and all are free of charge.

Ravens, Coyotes, and Scorpions!

To become a Junior Ranger, you must complete the requirements for your age group in the Junior Ranger Activity Booklet. You can get a booklet at any of the visitor centers or museums on the south or North Rims, including Canyon View Information Plaza, Yavapai Observation Station, Tusayan Museum, Desert View Information Center, and the North Rim Visitor Center.

Requirements for completion include writing down your observations and impressions, writing poems, answering questions about the park, and attending a free program led by a park ranger. This is a year-round program. There are different Junior Ranger Awards for these age groups:

- Ages 4 to 7: Raven Award
- Ages 8 to 10: Coyote Award
- Ages 11 and up: Scorpion Award

When you complete the requirements, bring the activity booklet to any visitor center or ranger station. A ranger will review your booklet, and issue an Official Grand Canyon Junior Ranger Certificate and Badge. Take your Junior Ranger Certificate to any park bookstore, and you can buy a sew-on patch to go with your Junior Ranger Award.

Phantom Rattler Junior Ranger

This is a special program for kids age 4 to 14. Only kids who ride mules or hike to Phantom Ranch at the bottom of the Grand Canyon can become Phantom Rattler Junior Rangers. After getting to Phantom Ranch, complete the activities in the Junior Ranger Booklet.

Booklets are available at the Phantom Ranch Ranger Station, the canteen, or the campground. After completing the activities in the booklet, you'll receive your Junior Ranger Badge, Patch, and Certificate from a ranger at Phantom Ranch. This program is available all year.

Junior Ranger Dynamic Earth Adventure Hike

Available from mid-June through mid-August, kids 8 to 14 can join a park ranger on a hike down the Hermit Trail. Up to two miles round-trip, this is a strenuous hike, so bring water and sunscreen and wear good hiking shoes.

The Adventure Hike begins at 9:00 AM at the Hermits Rest Bell, next to the Hermits Rest Shuttle Stop at the west end of Hermit Road. Board the Hermit Shuttle at the west end of Grand Canyon Village by 8:00 AM so you'll be on time.

After completing the 2-1/2-hour program, you'll be eligible to buy a Junior Ranger Adventure Hike patch. This program also satisfies the ranger activity requirement for the Junior Ranger Activity Booklet.

Junior Ranger Discovery Pack

This program is for kids 8 to 14 and their families. Young naturalists attend a 1-1/2-hour ranger-led program, which meets at Park Headquarters at 9:00 AM mid-June through Labor Day weekend. A park ranger will help kids and their families learn to use the tools in the Discovery Pack, which include binoculars, a hand lens, a journal, and field guides.

After the talk, families take the Discovery Pack with them while they explore the park for the day, completing the journal as they discover plants, animals, and birds. At the end of the day, return the Discovery Pack to a ranger, who will review the Discovery Pack Field Journal. This program also satisfies the ranger activity requirement for the Junior Ranger Activity Booklet.

North Rim Junior Ranger Discovery Pack

A Junior Ranger Discovery Pack program is also offered on the North Rim during the summer months. Check the North Rim Guide for information: http://www.nps.gov/grca/planyourvisit/

Junior Ranger Family Programs

These programs fulfill the requirement to participate in one ranger-led activity for the Raven, Coyote, or Scorpion Junior Ranger badges. They are offered from June through August.

Storytime Adventure

For kids from 2 to 6 years, this program is held on the lawn behind El Tovar Hotel from 1:30 to 2:00 PM daily, June 8 through September 1. A park ranger will read from his or her favorite Grand Canyon children's books, and require active audience participation.

Way Cool Stuff for Kids and Kids Rock!

Both programs are geared for kids from ages 6 to 12. Way Cool Stuff for Kids starts at 4:00 PM at the Shrine of the Ages parking lot A, and runs June through September 1.

Kids Rock! starts at the same place at 10:00 AM and runs June through August 16. Each program lasts one hour. Come prepared to have fun and learn something new! Previous topics have included:

- Bizarre Bats

- Amazing Mountain Lions

- Fire in a Forest

- Water in Our World

- Archeology
- Tremendous Trees
- Animal Tracking
- Astronomy
- Arts and Crafts

Photography

The virtue of the camera is not the power it has to transform the photographer into an artist, but the impulse it gives him to keep on looking - and looking. -Brooks Atkinson

Thundershower over eastern Grand Canyon

Why Didn't my Photo Come Out?

Many visitors to the Grand Canyon arrive after a drive up from I-40 and spend just a few hours at the rim, often during the middle of the day during the summer. The sun is high in the sky and floods the canyon with harsh light that washes out the colorful rock formations.

It's Not Your Equipment

Though the features on pro or semi-pro single lens reflex cameras are designed for versatility and flexibility in many different shooting situations, you can make stunning photographs with modest equipment as long as you understand its limitations. All but the cheapest point-and shoot-cameras have computer-designed lenses that are remarkably sharp. And you don't need a lot of megapixels either. Large posters can be made from five megapixel images.

Seeing the Light

The human eye is a remarkable instrument. It is far more sensitive to light than any camera and also has an extremely sophisticated processor- the brain. The brain processes what we see into what we expect to see, based on what we've already experienced. This means we don't see the strong blue cast to the mid-day light on someone's face caused by the strong blue light from the open sky. We also don't see that scraggly tree branch sticking into our picture when we take it, only the towering rock temple dominating the frame.

Composition in Thirds

The placement of objects within your photo should create a pattern that is pleasing to the eye and draw the viewer into the image. Remember the rule of thirds, which states that major objects such as people, trees, rock formations, or the horizon should be placed one-third of the way in from the edge of the frame rather than in the center. Centered subjects make for dull photos. Action subjects such as hikers or cyclists should be positioned at the one-third point and should be moving into the remaining two-thirds of the frame. In other words, give them space.

Simplify

When composing your shot, eliminate distractions. Include as little in the frame as you can and still tell the story that you're trying to convey to your viewers. Move closer to your subject or use a telephoto lens or setting. Watch out for wide-angle lenses or settings. Used carefully, wide-angle lenses can create breathtaking images that sweep the viewer from intimate detail in the foreground to broad landscapes in the background, but they can also be loaded with irrelevant clutter.

Golden Light

Experienced landscape photographers know about the golden hours, the hour after sunrise and the hour before sunset when the sun is low to the horizon and the light is filtered by the atmosphere into soft, warm tones. At the Grand Canyon, rock formations leap into three dimensions and seem to glow with inner fire. Shadows and haze fill the depths and add an aura of mystery.

During the summer, you'll have to rise early or stay out late to catch the golden hours. During the spring and fall when the days are shorter, it's less work to get out during the golden hours. And even the mid day light is softer due to the lower sun angle. Winter is one of the best times to photograph the Grand Canyon. The sun is at its lowest and snow on the rims and terraces brings out the colors and relief of the canyon to a remarkable degree.

Sunrise and Sunset Calculator:
http://aa.usno.navy.mil/data/docs/RS_OneDay.php

Where to Shoot

If your time is limited, walk to Mather Point from the Canyon View Information Plaza. Then try walking east along the Rim Trail, and shoot back toward Mather Point itself. A shot of the long promontory with people crowding the guard rails is especially effective early in the morning. Another option is to walk the Rim Trail from El Tovar Hotel east toward Yavapai Point. You'll get a variety of views and lots of people for interest. As the view faces mainly northwest until you get to Yavapai Point, this section of the Rim Trail has the best light late from afternoon until sunset.

South Rim

For sunrise, try Pima, Mohave, Hopi, Mather, Yaki, Moran, and Lipan points. For sunset, consider Powell, Trailview, Yaki, Grandview, and Lipan points. Yaki Point is good for shots of hikers on the upper Kaibab Trail. And don't forget the many historic buildings in Grand Canyon Village, including El Tovar Hotel, Bright Angel Lodge, and the old railway station.

North Rim

Bright Angel Point, the most popular viewpoint on the North Rim, is one of the worst for photography. Fortunately, Point Imperial, Cape Royal, and Angels Window more than make up for it. Point Imperial offers a close view of Mount Hayden and the cliff-bound head of Nankoweap Creek and is a good place for sunrise. Cape Royal is also best at sunrise and early in the day. Nearby Angels Window viewpoint is especially effective at sunset when the setting sun lights up the foreground buttes and the Palisades of the Desert to the east.

Backcountry

I'll admit I'm prejudiced, but limiting your photography to the rim viewpoints that are accessible by paved road barely lets you scratch the surface of the Grand Canyon. If you have the time and a high clearance vehicle, visits to backcountry viewpoints such as the South Bass Trailhead, Point Sublime, Fire Point, and Toroweap will pay off in dramatic shots taken from unusual perspectives.

Get Physical

To really explore the canyon photographically you have to explore it physically, which means hiking the trails and running the river. On the river with a raft to carry your gear, you can carry a lot of equipment but you won't want to endanger an expensive single lens reflex in the whitewater. One of the new waterproof, submersible point-and-shoots will let you get some great shots.

Day Hikes

You can day hike the upper parts of some of the trails from the rims and get to some interesting vantage points. Good places to start are the South Kaibab Trail to O'Neill Butte, the Grandview Trail to Horseshoe Mesa, and the Hermit Trail to Santa Maria Spring or Dripping Spring. On the North Rim, try the Transcept Trail.

Gear for Backpacking

Of course, really getting into the Grand Canyon on foot requires backpacking for two or more days. Because of weight, you can't carry much photo gear. One of the waterproof point-and-shoots makes a great backpacking camera. Or, as I generally prefer, you can carry a lightweight single lens reflex camera body (these are often classed as semi-pro cameras) and one of the new wide-range zoom lenses. Some of these cameras are now moisture and dust-sealed, a feature formerly available only on the heavy pro cameras.

Batteries and Storage Cards

Unless you'll have access to a charger and a computer or image storage device every day, make certain you have enough memory cards and fully charged batteries to last the trip. Memory cards are cheap, so there's no excuse for running out of space. Camera batteries are not cheap but current cameras are much easier on batteries than older models. You can greatly extend battery life by turning off the LCD monitor and using the viewfinder, if your camera has one. Also, turn off instant review and use the play button to selectively review photos as needed. In camp, resist the urge to edit your photos on the camera, unless you know you have plenty of battery power.

Commercial Photography

Commercial photography or videography involving props, models, professional crews and casts, or set dressings requires a permit. Personal or professional photography involving no more than a tripod and that doesn't disrupt other visitors does not require a permit or a fee in any national park.

Commercial Photography Permits: http://1.usa.gov/LWSvr

Mule Trips

Keep your eyes on the stars, and your feet on the ground. - Theodore Roosevelt

Mule party with Teddy Roosevelt at the head

The famous Grand Canyon mules are an experience many visitors just cannot miss. You can choose a day trip through the rim forest to The Abyss overlook west of Grand Canyon village. Or, if you want the classic Grand Canyon mule trip, ride the mules down the Bright Angel Trail and spend the night at Phantom Ranch at the bottom of the canyon. Xanterra, a park concessionaire operating by permit from the National Park Service, operates mule trips on Grand Canyon trails. For further information about mule trips, see Xanterra's website: www.grandcanyonlodges.com/mule-trips-716.html, or call 888-297-2757 or 303-297-2757.

River Running

We have an unknown distance yet to run, an unknown river to explore. What falls there are, we know not; what rocks beset the channel, we know not; what walls ride over the river, we know not. Ah, well! we may conjecture many things. -John Wesley Powell

Rafters in Middle Granite Gorge

Running the Colorado River through the Grand Canyon is a superb way to explore the canyon's backcountry, and floating the river with modern equipment is safe and easy. There are many excellent day hikes from the river that take you to places that are very difficult to reach from the rims.

Commercial River Trips

You can go on a commercial river trip with a river company operating under permit from the National Park Service. On these trips, professional river guides conduct the river trip which are a half-day to 18 days in length. Most commercial trips are motorized, but some companies offer oar-powered trips. If you have the time, oar-powered trips are the best, because you get to experience both the thrill of the whitewater and the awesome natural quiet of the Grand Canyon on the calm sections of the river between the rapids.

Reservations

To participate in a commercial river trip, make reservations with one of the river companies.

One Day Trips

Half- and full-day river trips start from Lees Ferry at the head of Marble Canyon, and float through lower Glen Canyon, the section of the Colorado River between Glen Canyon Dam and Lees Ferry. While not part of Grand Canyon, Glen Canyon is visually stunning, and there is no white water on this trip. For more information, see Colorado River Discovery's website: www.raftthecanyon.com, or call 888-522-6644 or 928-645-9175.

Other one day river trips start from Diamond Creek in the western Grand Canyon and end at Grand Canyon West. For information on these whitewater trips, see the Grand Canyon West website: http://www.grandcanyonwest.com/rafting.php, or call 888-868-9378 or 928-769-2230.

Three to 18 Day River Trips

These river trips all launch from Lees Ferry at the head of Marble Canyon. While the oar-powered rafts, motorized rafts, or dories float the entire length of the Grand Canyon to Lake Mead, trip participants can run shorter segments of the Colorado River by hiking the South Kaibab Trail to join or leave a river trip at Phantom Ranch in the eastern canyon.

Another option is to be picked up or dropped off by helicopter at Whitmore Wash in the western canyon. Flights from Whitmore Wash take river runners to Bar Ten Ranch, a private, working cattle ranch, where visitors may stay overnight and then fly out from the ranch airstrip.

Commercial River Companies

For information on river trips starting from Lees Ferry, contact one of the commercial outfitters:

Aramark-Wilderness River Adventures, P.O. Box 717, Page, AZ 86040; 800-992-8022, 928-645-3296, FAX 928-645-6113

Arizona Raft Adventures, Inc., 4050-F E. Huntington Drive, Flagstaff, AZ 86004; 800-786-RAFT, 928-526-8200, FAX 928-526-8246

Arizona River Runners, Inc., P.O. Box 47788, Phoenix, AZ 85068-7788; 800-477-7238, 602-867-4866, FAX 602-867-2174

Canyon Explorations/Canyon Expeditions, P.O. Box 310, Flagstaff, AZ 86002; 800-654-0723, 928-774-4559, FAX 928-774-4655

Canyoneers, Inc., P.O. Box 2997, Flagstaff, AZ 86003; 800-525-0924, 928-526-0924, FAX 928-527-9398

Colorado River & Trail Expeditions, Inc., P.O. Box 57575, Salt Lake City, UT 84157-0575; 800-253-7328, 801-261-1789, FAX 801-268-1193

Diamond River Adventures, Inc., P.O. Box 1300, Page, AZ 86040; 800-343-3121, 928-645-8866, FAX 928-645-9536

Grand Canyon Discovery, Inc., 4050 E Huntington Drive, Flagstaff, AZ 86004; 800-786-7238, 928-526-8200, FAX 928-526-8246

Grand Canyon Dories, P.O. Box 216, Altaville, CA 95221; 800-877-3679, 209-736-0805, FAX 209-736-2902

Grand Canyon Expeditions Company, P.O. Box 0, Kanab, UT 84741; 800-544-2691, 435-644-2691

Hatch River Expeditions, Inc., HC 67-35, Marble Canyon, AZ 86036; 800-856-8966, 928-355-2241, FAX: 928-355-2266

Moki Mac River Expeditions, Inc., P.O. Box 71242, Salt Lake City, UT 84171-0242; 800-284-7280, 801-268-6667, FAX 801-262-0935

O.A.R.S. Grand Canyon, Inc., P.O. Box 67, Angels Camp, CA 95222; 800-346-6277, 209-736-2924, FAX 209-736-2902

Outdoors Unlimited, 6900 Townsend Winona Road, Flagstaff, AZ 86004; 800-637-7238, 928-526-4546, FAX 928-526-6185

Tour West, Inc., P.O. Box 333, Orem, UT 84059; 800-453-9107, 801-225-0755, FAX 801-225-7979

Western River Expeditions, Inc., 7258 Racquet Club Drive, Salt Lake City, UT 84121; 800-453-7450, 801-942-6669, FAX 801-942-8514

Private River Trips

If you have the experience and the equipment, you can organize a private river trip of 3 to 25 days in length. Private trips are almost always oar-powered. Remember that the Colorado River through Grand Canyon is a technical run with many large, difficult rapids, and that river conditions change radically with water levels.

Permits

Private river trips require a permit which is issued via a lottery system. The lottery is necessary because the demand for permits far exceeds the number of permits available.

Three to Five Day River Trips

The shortest private river trips launch from Diamond Creek, which is located in the western Grand Canyon on the Hualapai Indian Reservation. Permits are required from both the Hualapai Tribe, which owns the access road and put-in, and the National Park Service (the Colorado River is in the national park). For more information, see the National Park Service Diamond Creek website: www.nps.gov/grca/planyourvisit/overview-diamond-ck.htm

12 to 25 Day River Trips

These trips all launch from Lees Ferry at the head of Marble Canyon, and end at Diamond Creek in the western Grand Canyon, or at South Cove on Lake Mead below the Grand Canyon.

For more information on private trips starting from Lee's Ferry, see the park website, Private River Trips from Lees Ferry:
www.nps.gov/grca/planyourvisit/overview-lees-ferry-diamond-ck.htm

Support Companies for Private River Trips:
www.nps.gov/grca/planyourvisit/river_support.htm

Additional information on both commercial and private river trips can be found on the Park website: www.nps.gov/grca/planyourvisit/whitewater-rafting.htm

Air Tours

In wilderness I sense the miracle of life, and behind it our scientific accomplishments fade to trivia. -Charles A. Lindbergh

Tour helicopter over western Grand Canyon

Airplane and helicopter air tours over Grand Canyon are available from airports outside the national park. These operators offer air tours from Grand Canyon National Park Airport and other airports in the region:

Grand Canyon National Park Airport

Air Grand Canyon: www.airgrandcanyon.com, 800-247-4726 or 928-638-2686

Grand Canyon Airlines: www.grandcanyonairlines.com, 866-235-9422

Grand Canyon Helicopters: www.grandcanyonhelicoptersaz.com, 928-638-2764

Maverick Helicopters: www.maverickhelicopter.com, 888-261-4414

Papillon Helicopters: www.papillon.com, 888-635-7272 or 702-736-7243

Westwind Air Service: www.westwindairservice.com, 480-991-5557

Page

Westwind Air Service: www.westwindairservice.com, 928-645-2494

Las Vegas

Grand Canyon Helicopters: www.grandcanyonhelicoptersaz.com, 702-835-8477

Scenic Airlines: www.scenic.com, 800-634-6801

Phoenix

Westwind Air Service: www.westwindairservice.com, 480-991-5557

Sedona

Arizona Helicopter Adventures: www.azheli.com, 800-282-5151 or 928-282-0904

Sky Treks: www.skytreks.com, 928-282-6628

Scottsdale

Sky Treks: www.skytreks.com, 480-998-1675

Exploring The Canyon

The Park

National parks are the best idea we ever had. Absolutely American, absolutely democratic, they reflect us at our best rather than our worst. -Wallace Stegner

Eastern Grand Canyon

Much of the Grand Canyon is protected in Grand Canyon National Park and is managed by the National Park Service, a federal agency within the Department of the Interior. Part of the northwestern Grand Canyon is protected in Grand Canyon-Parashant National Monument, which is jointly managed by the National Park Service and the Bureau of Land Management, another agency of the Department of the Interior.

The southwestern quarter of the Grand Canyon lies within the Hualapai Indian Reservation. Lower Havasu Canyon and Great Thumb Mesa are part of the Havasupai Indian Reservation. The Navajo Indian Reservation lies adjacent to the east boundary of the national park.

Kaibab National Forest covers part of the Coconino Plateau south of the national park and part of the Kaibab Plateau north of the national park. The forest is managed by the U.S. Forest Service, a federal agency of the Department of Agriculture. Portions of Grand Canyon-Parashant National Monument and the Kaibab National Forest are National Wilderness areas.

Land Management

For the visitor to the Grand Canyon, the effect of these different managing agencies is that the rules change as you move into a different jurisdiction. Most of the national park is managed for preservation, but portions, mainly on the rims and at Phantom Ranch within the canyon, are managed to provide amenities for visitors. The national forest is managed for multiple uses, including logging, mining, and motorized recreation. Wilderness areas are managed to maintain their primitive character and motorized equipment is not allowed.

The two Indian reservations are managed by the tribes for the tribal members, which includes providing some access for visitors. For details on the history of the national park and the other management units, see People and the Canyon.

Is All of the Grand Canyon in the National Park?

Not quite. Grand Canyon National Park covers 1,218,376 acres (493,077 hectares). Grand Canyon runs generally east to west, and is bounded by the North and South Rims. Since 1975, the park has included all of the North Rim and about half of the South Rim, as well as Marble Canyon to the northeast. Most of the park's five million visitors spend their time at Grand Canyon Village and on the West Rim and Desert View drives. Grand Canyon Village is actually located along the east end of the South Rim and North Rim Village is at the east end of the North Rim. (See the map on page 3.)

Visitation and Amenities

Each year, four to five million people visit Grand Canyon National Park. Ninety percent of these visitors go to Grand Canyon Village on the South Rim. The South Rim has most of the park's amenities and is easiest to reach. About ten percent of park visitors go to the North Rim. Relatively few get to remote areas of the park, such as Toroweap or Point Sublime.

Colorado River

Other visitors float down the Colorado River from Lee's Ferry at the head of Marble Canyon on river trips lasting from a few days to several weeks. The river provides the easiest access to the wilderness backcountry of the Grand Canyon.

Trails

Two maintained trails provide access to the canyon itself from the Grand Canyon Village and North Rim Village areas. Another dozen or so unmaintained trails provide further access to the Grand Canyon's wilderness from points along the South Rim scenic drives, and from remote dirt roads on the North Rim. This trail network covers only a small portion of the park. Away from the trail network, all the hiking is cross-country which requires fitness and experience in desert hiking.

Park Backcountry

Access to most of the two rims, other than the Grand Canyon Village and North Rim Village areas, is by long, remote dirt roads, most of which are not maintained for passenger cars. Only those visitors who have appropriate high clearance vehicles and are equipped and experienced back-road desert travelers should attempt these roads.

Regulations

Within the national park, regulations have been designed to protect the park. In general, disturbance or removal of any natural object, plant, animal, or historic object or structure is prohibited, as is the possession of loaded firearms. Camping is allowed only in campgrounds. A permit is required for overnight or longer backpacking trips, for camping in the backcountry, and for river trips. See the Hiking and River Running chapters for details.

The Monument

The name of my Band is Cedar Band of Paiutes. My last name, Parashonts, means Elk or large deer standing in the water. I think the spelling of the Paiute word goes something like Pah-duee'. That is my family name on my grandparents' and mother's side. She was Paiute from Shivwits, as was my grandmother, Catherine Bonapart was from Shivwits also. My grandfather is Woots Parashonts, a Paiute born in Beaver County and lived in the Cedar area. I am registered under my grandfather's name with the Cedar Band of Paiutes. Our name comes from the newly created Parashonts National Monument down along the BLM Arizona Strip. That's where my family comes from. That is a little history on my name. Thanks for thinking of me and my family. You have honored me in a good way. -Travis Parashonts

Waterfall in a side canyon

If you want to explore a place that is well off the beaten path, Grand Canyon-Parashant National Monument is your destination. Encompassing a large portion of the Arizona Strip country north of the Grand Canyon, the monument includes the volcanic Uinkaret Mountains, the dramatic Hurricane Cliffs, and a portion of the northwest rim of the Grand Canyon. Four wilderness areas are included in the national monument; Paiute, Grand Wash Cliffs, Mount Trumbull, and Mount Logan wildernesses.

73

Former Grand Canyon National Monument

Not to be confused with the old Grand Canyon National Monument, which was incorporated into Grand Canyon National Park by Act of Congress in 1975, Grand Canyon-Parashant National Monument was created by presidential proclamation on January 11, 2000. President Theodore Roosevelt first used the Antiquities Act of 1906 to protect wildlife areas, forests, and scenic lands he thought should be preserved for all Americans.

Antiquities Act

Many of our major national parks and much of the national forest system were first protected by presidents using the Antiquities Act. Although the president and the Congress may both create national monuments, only Congress can create or rescind a national park or rescind a national monument. Presidents have used their power to create national monuments so wisely and effectively that Congress has never rescinded a presidential national monument.

Location

Grand Canyon-Parashant National Monument lies about 30 miles southwest of St. George, Utah, and is only accessible via long dirt roads. (See the map on page 3.) There are no services of any kind within the national monument. Visitors planning to explore the national monument should be experienced and equipped for remote desert travel. Most of the monument's roads are not maintained for passenger cars. It is recommended that you have a high clearance, four-wheel-drive vehicle. Carry plenty of food and water.

Grand Canyon-Parashant National Monument (NPS website):
www.nps.gov/para/index.htm

Grand Canyon-Parashant National Monument (BLM website):
www.blm.gov/az/st/en/prog/blm_special_areas/natmon/gcp.html

South Rim

Wilderness is not a luxury but a necessity of the human spirit. -Edward Abbey

Yavapai Point looking east toward Wotans Throne and Vishnu Temple

Most Grand Canyon visitors go to the South Rim, which includes the village of Tusayan and Grand Canyon National Park Airport outside the park, and Grand Canyon Village and Desert View inside the park. The South Rim also features many rim viewpoints accessible from the Desert View Drive and Hermit Road.

Free Shuttle Buses

Free shuttle bus service operated by the park provides transportation around Grand Canyon Village, the Hermit Road, to Yaki Point and the Kaibab Trailhead, and to Tusayan and the airport.

Amenities

The South Rim has most of the Grand Canyon's amenities, including restaurants, lodging, and camping both within the park and outside of the park. Seasonal park shuttles operate between the airport, Tusayan, and Grand Canyon Village, and taxi service is available all year. Market Plaza features a general store which sells groceries as well as camping, hiking, and backpacking equipment. Equipment rentals are also available. There is also a bank and ATM, self-service laundry, showers, and post office.

Trails

The Grand Canyon's main trails, the Kaibab and Bright Angel, start from the South Rim, as do many of the unmaintained backcountry trails.

When to Visit

The South Rim is open all year. Summer is the most popular time to visit and the high elevation of the South Rim, 7,000 feet, keeps the weather mild. Days are warm and the nights cool. Late summer typically brings afternoon thunderstorms which often create dramatic skies and stunning sunsets. Fall is the best time to visit- nights are crisp, often dropping below freezing, but the days are pleasant and the weather stable.

Winter is the least popular and often the most rewarding time to visit the South Rim, as the occasional snow storm drapes the canyon terraces with snow, emphasizing the colors and forms of the canyon. Winter nights are cold and the days chilly, but there are long sunny periods between the occasional storms. Spring has changeable weather with windy storms and even some snow alternating with calm, mild periods.

Getting Around the South Rim

Use the Free Shuttles

From March through October, roads and parking in the Grand Canyon Village area are congested. The best way to get around the village is via the free shuttle bus, which operates year-round in the village, to the Kaibab Trailhead and Yaki Point, and seasonally along Hermit Road and to Tusayan and the airport.

Park Away From the Rim

It is easiest to find a parking spot near the Backcountry Information Center at the west end of the village, or near Park Headquarters at the east end of the village. There are also large parking lots at Market Plaza and Canyon View Information Plaza, but these tend to fill early.

Exploring the South Rim

Canyon View Information Plaza and Mather Point

The best place to start your visit to the South Rim is at Canyon View Information Plaza, located at the east end of Grand Canyon Village. Indoor and outdoor exhibits explain the geology and history of the Grand Canyon. You can buy books, DVDs, and souvenirs at the Books and More bookstore located in the plaza.

Mather Point

From Canyon View Information Plaza, you can follow a handicap-accessible paved trail a quarter mile out to spectacular Mather Point, the most visited and photographed viewpoint at the Grand Canyon. Mather Point is especially scenic at sunrise and sunset.

Canyon View Information Plaza

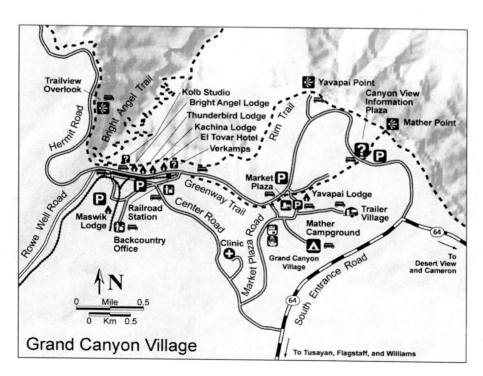

Grand Canyon Village

Ranger Programs

Free programs led by park rangers are a great way to get to know the canyon. The programs include guided walks, campfire talks, geology, and special subjects.

Rim Trail

A paved, accessible section of the Rim Trail runs from Bright Angel Lodge at the west end of the village to Yavapai Point. The Rim Trail then continues east to Mather Point and Pipe Creek View. Starting from either Bright Angel Lodge or El Tovar Hotel, the Rim Trail provides continuously changing views into Garden Creek Canyon and Pipe Creek.

Bright Angel Lodge

This rustic lodge, built of timber and native stone, was designed by architect Mary Colter and opened in 1935. Her intention, under the direction of the Santa Fe Railroad, was to create a hotel that would be a lower cost alternative to El Tovar Hotel. Colter's signature as an architect was to incorporate local flavor into her buildings. Bucky O'Neill Cabin was one of the first buildings in Grand Canyon Village, and Mary Colter not only preserved the cabin but incorporated its design into the design of Bright Angel Lodge. Another historic structure that she preserved and used for inspiration is the Red Horse Station, which was used as the post office for many years. Both buildings are still in use today.

Bright Angel Lodge is located west of El Tovar just a few feet from the South Rim and the Bright Angel Trailhead. See the Lodging link under Activities for lodging and dining information.

Bright Angel Lodge

Kolb Studio

This historic structure, perched just below the South Rim, was the home and studio of the Kolb brothers, early photographers and cinematographers of the Grand Canyon. Completely restored, the studio now houses a bookstore and a free Grand Canyon art exhibit.

Emory and Ellsworth Kolb arrived at the South Rim just after the turn of the 20th century. By 1903, they were operating a photographic studio near the head of the Bright Angel Trail. They took pictures of mule parties on the trail, developed them in a makeshift darkroom in a cave, and sold the prints to the tourists. In 1904 they built a two-story studio on a rock shelf blasted out of the Kaibab limestone just below the rim.

In 1912 the brothers ran the Colorado River through the Grand Canyon and made the first movie of a Grand Canyon river trip. After a national promotional tour, they returned to the Grand Canyon and added a three-story annex to the studio for living quarters and a gallery. The brothers began showing the movie in 1915. After Ellsworth's death, Emory Kolb continued to run the movie every day until his own death in 1976.

Kolb Studio

Lookout Studio

Designed by Mary Colter and built by the Santa Fe Railroad in 1914 for the purpose of competing with Kolb Studio, Lookout Studio is on the edge of the rim in front of Bright Angel Lodge. Colter employed her design philosophy of using local inspiration by constructing the building from native stone and giving it an irregular roof line so that it would blend into the rim. It now serves as a bookstore and has high-powered telescopes on the observation deck so that visitors can view the Grand Canyon in detail.

Lookout Studio

El Tovar Hotel

One of the Fred Harvey hotels built in conjunction with the Santa Fe Railroad, El Tovar is a classic log cabin style hotel and was built in 1905. It is located just a few feet from the South Rim. El Tovar was designed by Charles Whittlesey, the chief architect for the railroad. As the Santa Fe Railroad extended lines to western national parks, the railroad commissioned a series of hotels at the parks in order to ensure that rail travelers would have a world class hotel waiting for them. At the same time, the railroad wanted to preserve the unique American wilderness feel of the setting, so they designed the lodges in a particular rustic style that has become known as National Park Service Rustic. Although El Tovar has been remodeled and the guest rooms updated several times (most recently in 2008), the building still retains its rustic character.

As the premier place to stay at the Grand Canyon, the hotel has hosted many famous people over the years, including Ferdinand Foch, Gugliemo Marconi, George Bernard Shaw, Arthur Fiedler, and Presidents William Howard Taft and Theodore Roosevelt. Roosevelt was so inspired by his visits to the Grand Canyon that he established Grand Canyon National Game Preserve and Grand Canyon National Monument by presidential proclamation, which led to the creation of the national park.

See the Lodging chapter for lodging and dining information.

El Tovar Hotel

Yavapai Point

Verkamps Visitor Center

This building, located next to El Tovar Hotel, was built in 1905 by John Verkamp and was operated as a curio shop until 2008. Verkamps was the most famous souvenir shop at the Grand Canyon and was a must-visit location for many park visitors. It is now a park visitor center and bookstore specializing in the pioneer history of Grand Canyon Village and the experience of living and working on the rim of the Grand Canyon.

Verkamp first arrived at Grand Canyon Village in 1898 and began selling souvenirs from a tent. Business was slow and he moved to Flagstaff until the railroad reached the South Rim and tourism increased dramatically. Verkamp returned to the Grand Canyon and opened his curio business in his new building in 1906.

One of the reasons that Verkamps was so popular was the family tradition of service to the customer as well as their employees. Many of their items for sale were purchased from local artists, and employees were trained in the history and significance of the art work so they could pass that knowledge on to the store's customers.

The Verkamp family was also heavily involved in the Grand Canyon Village community. They helped develop Grand Canyon School and actively supported the Shrine of the Ages and the community library. They also supported the local Boy Scouts and helped found the local Rotary Club.

Yavapai Point

Reachable by car, the Village Shuttle, and the Rim Trail, Yavapai Point features views of Bright Angel Creek to the west and Pipe Creek to the east. Look for the patch of cottonwood trees and buildings along Garden Creek marking the ranger station and campground at Indian Garden along the Bright Angel Trail. A small museum and book store, Yavapai Observation Station offers exhibits explaining the fascinating geology of the Grand Canyon.

Yavapai Point features a Web cam and is an air quality monitoring station for the park. Visitors to national parks expect to see clear, unpolluted air, but unfortunately national parks do not exist under a sealed dome. They are part of the regional environment, which in the Southwest includes such nearby pollution sources as coal-fired power plants in the Four Corners area, various mining operations, and the large metropolitan areas of Phoenix, Las Vegas, and Los Angeles.

Part of the purpose of the national park air monitoring program is to determine the source of pollutants by studying the pollution particles in the air. The nature of the particles identifies the source, and this information is used by government agencies and private enterprise to reduce the amount of pollutants at their sources.

Within the park, the Park Service reduces pollution by operating an alternative fuel vehicle fleet for administrative purposes. The park also operates a free year-round shuttle bus system throughout the Grand Canyon Village area and to Kaibab Trailhead and Yaki Point. Except in the winter, free shuttles also run along the Hermit Road and to Tusayan and the airport.

Mather Point

Accessible via a quarter-mile trail from Canyon View Information Plaza, Mather Point is the first view of the canyon for many visitors. The viewpoint itself is located at the tip of a spectacular fin of Kaibab limestone which projects out into the canyon. Mather Point is an excellent location for sunrise photos. Walk east along the paved Rim Trail to get a view of Mather Point and the sheer, sunlit cliffs below standing in sharp contrast to the early morning shadows of the canyon depths in the background.

To the east, you can see the upper portion of the South Kaibab Trail. The initial portion of the trail where it descends through the Kaibab limestone rim cliffs is hidden from view in a north facing alcove, but then the trail comes into view as it descends below Yaki Point along the sloping terrace eroded from the Toroweap formation. As the trail comes out onto the red slopes of the Hermit shale, it swings around the east side of O'Neill Butte and disappears from view.

Pipe Creek is visible below as well as a portion of the 72-mile long Tonto Trail winding along the greenish-gray shale slopes of the Tonto Plateau. This section of the Tonto Trail is in better shape and more visible from above because it has been used several times as part of the main rim to river route on the Bright Angel Trail. The original route of the Bright Angel Trail was down upper Garden Creek, along the Tonto Plateau across Pipe Creek, and then down to the Colorado River along what is now the lower South Kaibab Trail. After the River Trail was completed to connect lower Pipe Creek to the two footbridges across the Colorado River at the mouth of Bright Angel Creek and the foot of the Kaibab Trail, the Tonto Trail fell into disuse except by backcountry hikers. It was temporarily used as the main route again when the lower Bright Angel Trail in Pipe Creek was closed for reconstruction for several years.

The Plateau Point Trail is also visible leaving the green, spring-fed oasis of Indian Garden and heading out to a viewpoint just west of Garden Creek. Plateau Point is unusually flat for the Tonto plateau and part of the trail crosses a landing strip used

August 8, 1922 by RV Thomas and Ellsworth Kolb to land a plane and take off again. Emory Kolb hiked down to the airstrip to photograph the event.

To the north, on the far side of Granite Gorge, you'll note Bright Angel Canyon. Phantom Ranch, the only resort at the bottom of the Grand Canyon, and Bright Angel Campground are located at the mouth of Bright Angel Creek just above the Colorado River on the North Kaibab Trail. The trail continues most of the way up Bright Angel Creek before climbing up Roaring Springs Canyon to North Rim Village.

Pipe Creek Vista

This viewpoint looks down onto Pipe Creek, the major canyon between the Kaibab Trail and the Bright Angel Trail and can be reached by car from the Desert View Drive or via the Kaibab Trail Shuttle. Pick up the Kaibab Trail Shuttle at the Canyon View Information Plaza. This is also the eastern trailhead for the Rim Trail, which runs west from Pipe Creek Vista past Mather Point to Grand Canyon Village and on to Hermits Rest.

Pipe Creek Vista

Yaki Point

Use the Kaibab Trail Shuttle to reach this viewpoint overlooking the Kaibab Trail descending past red O'Neill Butte. Since private cars are not allowed, Yaki Point is a quiet place to watch the sunrise or sunset.

The view includes much of the upper South Kaibab Trail. Some visitors wonder why this popular trail was located four miles east of Grand Canyon Village. The answer is that it was built by the Park Service as an alternate route to the Bright Angel Trail, which was under private ownership in 1919 when the national park was created.

O'Neill Butte is a major landmark along the Kaibab Trail. The red cliffs of the butte are carved from the upper sandstone layers of the Supai formation. The butte is named after Bucky O'Neill, a member of Theodore Roosevelt's Rough Riders.

Cremation Canyon lies to the east of the Kaibab Trail and is one of the sites where the famous split-twig figurines of the Grand Canyon have been discovered. These ancient artifacts were made from a single twig split down the middle and folded into animal shapes. Willow was most often used due to the wood's flexibility. Dating from 2,000 to 4,000 years old, split-twig figurines are found in remote, undisturbed caves where they are protected from the weather. You can see some examples of these remarkable artifacts at the Tusayan Museum on Desert View Drive.

Yaki Point

Hermit Road

The Hermit Road and the mileage log start at the west end of Grand Canyon Village and follows the canyon rim to the west for 7 miles. The road ends at Hermits Rest and the Hermit Trailhead. The Rim Trail also follows the rim out to Hermits Rest.

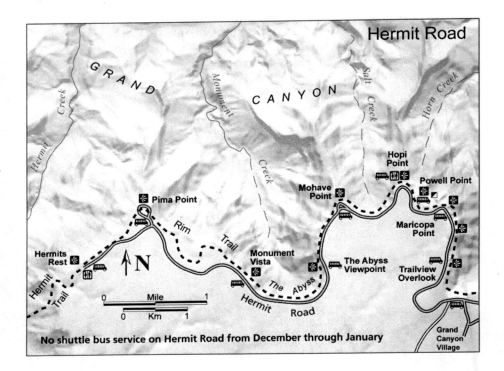

0.0 Hermit/Village Shuttle Transfer Stop

Private cars are not allowed on the Hermit Road except during the winter. The shuttle is a great way to travel the Hermit Road because it stops at all the viewpoints. You can spend as much time at the viewpoints as you wish and catch the shuttle to the next one, or walk the Rim Trail between shuttle stops. The mileage log starts at the Hermit Shuttle Stop, located at the Bright Angel Trailhead at the west end of Grand Canyon Village. The Village Shuttle also stops here, allowing you to transfer between shuttles.

Another great way to enjoy the Hermit Road is by bicycle during spring, summer and fall when the free shuttle is operating. Because private cars are not allowed except during the winter, riding the Hermit Road is a quiet and relaxing experience. The shuttle buses have bicycle racks, so you can ride the Hermit Road one way and take the shuttle the other. The best way to do this is to take the shuttle to Hermits Rest and ride back to Grand Canyon Village, which avoids the climb from the Hermit/Village Shuttle Stop.

86

Before boarding the shuttle, have a look off the rim. You are standing at the head of Garden Creek, the canyon containing the Bright Angel Trail. You are also standing on the Bright Angel Fault. The rim to your left has been raised about 180 feet higher than the rim beneath your feet. The resulting fracture weakened the rocks and allowed water to carve out the canyon below you. The fault also broke down the Redwall limestone cliff at the head of Garden Creek and created a route that native Americans used to descend the canyon. The same break was used when the modern Bright Angel Trail was constructed. The Bright Angel Fault continues southwest across the Coconino Plateau behind you, and also to the northeast across the Grand Canyon onto the North Rim. Bright Angel Canyon follows the Bright Angel Fault north of the Colorado River, and the North Kaibab Trail in turn follows Bright Angel Canyon.

1.2 Trailview Overlook

Trailview Overlook looks to the east over upper Garden Creek and Grand Canyon Village. You are seemingly looking straight down on the Bright Angel Trail as it switchbacks down the break in the cliffs caused by the Bright Angel Fault. Most Grand Canyon trails and routes take advantage of such fault breaks.

The Redwall limestone is an especially formidable obstacle. This massive limestone formation is about halfway between rim and river and persists throughout the length of the Grand Canyon. The Redwall limestone forms about 1,000 miles of cliffs that are uniformly about 550 feet high throughout the Canyon. Along the length of the Grand Canyon there are only about 200 known breaks where the Redwall limestone can be descended without technical climbing gear. Although most of these breaks are mainly used by wildlife and the occasional backcountry hiker, all of the Grand Canyon's trails except for the North and South Kaibab trails use natural fault breaks in the Redwall limestone.

Snow defines the terraces of the Canyon as seen from Trailview Overlook

1.7 Maricopa Point

Maricopa Point overlooks the inactive Orphan Lode Mine, operated from 1891 to 1967. Originally a copper mine, the Orphan Lode began exploiting uranium deposits in the 1950s. Although the park now owns the mine, environmental cleanup has been difficult, which highlights the hazards associated with uranium mining in the region.

The Battleship, a distinctive butte in the reddish Supai formation, is prominent below to the northeast. For many years, employees of the Fred Harvey Company, which operated the hotels and concessions on the South Rim, would climb The Battleship on the Fourth of July and replace the American flag that flew on the summit. As Grand Canyon summits go, the Battleship is an easy climb. It can be reached from the Bright Angel Trail and a short cross-country hike along the terraces in the Supai formation. Easy rock scrambling leads to the summit. Still, it is not a hike for the inexperienced. Stick to the Bright Angel and Kaibab trails for your first hike into the canyon.

2.2 Powell Point

Powell Point commemorates the two historic voyages of exploration down the Colorado River through Grand Canyon undertaken by Major John Wesley Powell and his boat crews in 1869 and 1871. Major Powell named the Grand Canyon and was the first to explore and map the region. Before Powell's first voyage, the Grand Canyon region was marked "unexplored" on maps. Many predicted that Powell's voyage would end in disaster because the Colorado River would go over a waterfall that could not be portaged or run, and the expedition would be trapped in a canyon that could not be climbed.

Powell, as a trained geologist, was certain that there would be no waterfalls in the canyons of the Green and Colorado Rivers that he proposed to run. Waterfalls are very young landscape features (Niagara Falls is less than 10,000 years old) and Powell knew that the Grand Canyon is millions of years old. He did assume that there would be ferocious rapids along the river, so he ordered strong oak boats. Although his boats didn't turn out to be the best river craft, they did the job. Powell and his men ran the river system from Green River, Wyoming, without any serious injuries or loss of life.

The Battleship from Powell Point

Powell brought along a photographer and an artist, so his expeditions not only produced the first detailed maps of the region, but also the first images of the Grand Canyon of the Colorado River, as he named the canyon.

2.4 Hopi Point

Hopi Point is a good place to catch the sunset glow on the canyon walls to the north and east and also offers views of the Colorado River. Dana Butte forms the end of the Redwall limestone point almost directly to the north. There are restrooms at Hopi Point.

The view from Hopi Point is the classic eastern Grand Canyon panorama. The upper two-thirds of the canyon is a sequence of cliffs formed in the hard Kaibab limestone, Supai formation, and Redwall limestone. Narrow terraces between the cliffs are formed on the softer rocks of the Toroweap formation, Hermit shale, and shale layers in the Supai formation.

About 3,500 feet below the rim, a major terrace forms on the Bright Angel shale. This shale layer is much thicker than the shale layers above and below, so the soft rock erodes easily and undermines the Muav and Redwall limestone cliffs above. The cliffs recede to form a wide terrace known as the Tonto Plateau. This plateau is about 1,200

Hopi Point

feet above the Colorado River and is the dominant terrace in the eastern third of the Grand Canyon, which is the portion visible from the Hermit Road.

3.1 Mohave Point

Mohave Point is a good spot for canyon sunrises, as it looks north and west at rock faces lit by the rising sun. It also offers views of the Tonto Plateau, Granite Gorge, and the Colorado River.

While most of the trails in the Grand Canyon descend from rim to river, several trails traverse the terraces in the canyon. The best known such trail is the Tonto Trail, which winds along the Tonto Plateau from Red Canyon on the east to Garnet Canyon on the west, a distance of 72 miles. The trail was originally built by prospectors but very little of the trail was actually constructed. Most of the trail was created from the repeated passage of miners and their pack animals. Some construction was done where the trail crossed side canyons. When prospecting ceased in the Grand Canyon after the creation of the national park, the Tonto Trail fell into disuse and was maintained mostly by wild burros, the feral descendants of the prospector's pack stock.

As you can see by looking down on the Tonto Plateau from Mohave Point, the Tonto Trail is anything but straight. The trail is constantly detouring around the heads of side canyons and side-side canyons as well as every little ravine. It spends some of its time out on the very edge of the gorge containing the Colorado River, but much of the time the Tonto Trail is back in the recesses of the canyons. Not so apparent from the rim viewpoints is the fact that the Tonto Plateau is anything but level. It only appears flat from above because of the extreme terrain above and below. While hiking

Mohave Point

the Tonto Trail you are constantly climbing and descending and winding around side canyons. It's definitely an exercise in patience. The best thing to do is take your time and enjoy the ever-changing views.

3.7 The Abyss

At The Abyss, the shale layers that normally form terraces between the upper cliffs are unusually thin, so the cliffs form a nearly sheer wall below the South Rim at the head of Monument Creek. This is a vivid example of how small variations in the rock layers can create major differences in the topography of the Grand Canyon. In fact, the upper cliffs of the Grand Canyon are so persistent and have so few breaks along the Hermit Road that there are no known routes from the rim to the Colorado River between the Bright Angel and Hermit trails.

5.2 Monument Creek Vista

Overlooking the headwaters of Monument Creek, this viewpoint and shuttle stop is also the trailhead for the Greenway Trail, a handicap-accessible trail following the old 1912 alignment of Hermit Road. Monument Creek features a permanent stream and has created a ferocious rapid where it meets the Colorado River.

Contrary to popular impressions, rapids along the Colorado River in the Grand Canyon are not the remnants of old waterfalls. Instead, every Grand Canyon rapid forms where debris has been washed down a side canyon into the river. When a heavy thundershower or prolonged rain falls into a side canyon, the resulting runoff quickly gathers speed as it descends the steep slopes of bare rock and sparsely vegetated soil. The ability of flowing water to carry sand, pebbles, cobbles, and boulders increases rapidly with the water's speed, enabling the flooding side canyon to carry large amounts of debris to the river. This debris forms a partial dam in the river. The river ponds up behind the dam and then gains speed over the submerged rocks, creating a rapid. Because the river flows much more slowly than the side canyon floods, it takes hundreds of years to wear away the boulders that created the rapid.

6.2 Pima Point

Pima Point looks down on Hermit Camp, the site of a major tourist camp operated on the edge of Hermit Creek on the Tonto Plateau. An aerial tramway once spanned the 4,000-foot space between Pima Point and Hermit Camp and was used to haul supplies to and from the site.

When Grand Canyon National Park was created in 1919, the present Grand Canyon Village was already the focus of tourist activity on the South Rim due to the arrival of the Santa Fe Railroad a few years before. The only problem was that there wasn't a freely accessible trail to the Colorado River. The Bright Angel Trail was still privately owned, and the owner charged an exorbitant fee for the use of his trail. Fred Harvey Company wanted to build a tourist camp below the rim, so they built the Hermit Road out to to the head of Hermit Canyon west of Grand Canyon Village, and then built the Hermit Trail down Hermit Creek to the Colorado River.

Hermit Camp was established on the Tonto Plateau just east of Hermit Creek. Tent cabins accommodated guests, and the camp was complete with running water and

Monument Creek Vista

even a Model T Ford that was sent down in pieces on the aerial tramway. Hermit Trail continued to the river along lower Hermit Creek, though little of the original construction has survived the periodic floods.

When the National Park Service gave up on buying the Bright Angel Trail and constructed the South Kaibab Trail as an alternate route to the river below Grand Canyon Village in the late 1920's, Fred Harvey Company opened a new tourist camp, Phantom Ranch, along lower Bright Angel Creek. When the North Kaibab Trail was completed, creating a trail across the Grand Canyon from Grand Canyon Village to North Rim Village, Phantom Ranch took over from Hermit Camp as the premier tourist camp within the canyon, and Hermit Camp was abandoned.

7.0 Hermits Rest

Hermit Road ends here, at the small gift shop and snack bar occupying the historic building designed by famed Grand Canyon architect Mary Colter. Hermits Rest is also the trailhead for the Hermit Trail, originally built to access Hermit Creek. The Dripping Springs Trail connects the upper Hermit Trail to the upper Boucher Trail, and together with a segment of the Tonto Trail forms a loop hike very popular with backpackers. A rewarding day hike can be made down the upper Hermit Trail to Santa Maria Spring. The spring is not reliable but the view is.

Sunrise patterns from Pima Point

Desert View Drive

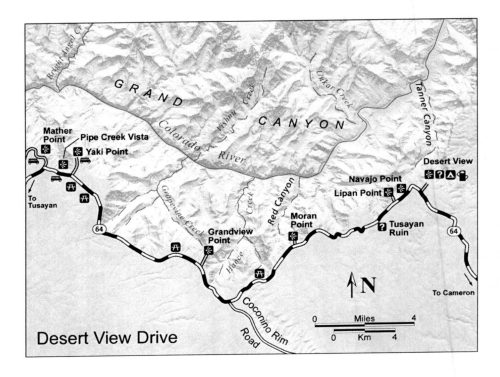

Desert View Drive

0.0 Intersection of South Rim and Desert View Drives

Desert View Drive and the mileage log start at the T-intersection on the South Rim Entrance Road, east of Canyon View Information Plaza and follows the South Rim 21 miles east to Desert View. In addition to the named viewpoints, there are several unnamed viewpoints and quiet picnic areas along the road.

0.7 Pipe Creek Vista

This viewpoint is on the left next to the road and can be reached by car or the free Kaibab Shuttle. Pick up the Kaibab Shuttle at the Canyon View Information Plaza. It is the first viewpoint after entering Desert View Drive from the South Rim Entrance Road. From here, you're looking down Pipe Creek. A section of the Tonto Trail is visible snaking along the Tonto Plateau about 3,000 feet below the rim. The original Bright Angel Trail used this section of the Tonto Trail as part of its route from rim to river. This is also the eastern trailhead for the Rim Trail. The Rim Trail follows the South Rim west to Hermits Rest at the end of the Hermit Road. There are shuttle bus stops at the major viewpoints along the Rim Trail, which lets you walk any part and then catch the shuttle.

1.2 Yaki Point and Kaibab Trailhead

The side road to Yaki Point and the South Kaibab Trailhead is accessible only via the Kaibab Trail Shuttle. Yaki Point offers a view of the upper South Kaibab Trail. This trail was built by the Park Service during the 1920's shortly after the creation of the national park to avoid tolls on the privately-owned Bright Angel Trail. Together with the North Kaibab Trail, the trail is the only maintained trail across the Grand Canyon form South Rim to North Rim. But the Kaibab Trail wasn't the first transcanyon trail. That honor goes to the South and North Bass trails, built by William Bass to reach his prospects and mine workings in the Bass Canyon and Shinumo Creek areas, far to the west of the Kaibab Trail. Like several other miners, Bass later used his trails to guide tourists. By ferrying his customers across the Colorado River in a boat or taking them across on a cableway, he could guide them from the South Rim to the North Rim and back.

8.8 Grandview Point

Well-named Grandview Point is not only the trailhead for the Grandview Trail but also one of the best viewpoints on the South Rim. The panoramic views overlook Horseshoe Mesa, Hance Canyon, and the Colorado River. This area was also the location of the first hotel at the rim of the Grand Canyon. Grandview Hotel was a log structure located southeast of Grandview Point along the rim. It was the primary destination for early visitors who arrived by stagecoach from Flagstaff or Williams. Grandview Hotel's only competition was from tent camps on the rim to the east and west. Once the railroad reached Grand Canyon Village in 1905 and El Tovar Hotel was completed in 1912, the Village area became the focus of tourism on the South Rim and Grandview Hotel was abandoned. Today little remains to mark the site except a few pieces of crockery.

Grandview Point

14.6 Moran Point

At Moran Point, you can clearly see the transition in the canyon's geology as the soft, colorful, tilted rocks of the Grand Canyon Supergroup, which make up the floor of the canyon to the east, give way to the hard, dark gray rocks of the Vishnu Schist, which forms Granite Gorge to the west.

The Grand Canyon Supergroup is not present throughout the Grand Canyon. These layers of rock were deposited on top of the Vishnu schist and then uplifted and faulted to form a major mountain range. Most of those mountains, and the Supergroup, were eroded away before the Tapeats sandstone was deposited on top of the Vishnu schist.

18.5 Tusayan Museum

Located off the south side of Desert View Drive between Moran and Lipan points, this small museum has exhibits and books that explain the nearby ruin from the Pueblo period. An easy trail loops around the ruin and there are restrooms and a small picnic area.

Tusayan Ruin

Moran Point

19.7 Lipan Point

Located on a promontory projecting out over the canyon, Lipan Point has fine views of the colorful geology of the eastern canyon. The floor of the canyon to the northeast is dominated by the soft, colorful shales and sandstones of the Grand Canyon Supergroup, a tilted layer of ancient rocks which is best exposed at the eastern end of the Grand Canyon. The Colorado River meanders through this landscape as it passes Tanner and Unkar rapids. Lipan Point is also the trailhead for the Tanner Trail, a steep, unmaintained trail which descends past Escalante and Cardenas buttes to Tanner Rapids at the Colorado River.

Escalante and Cardenas buttes from Lipan Point

20.8 Navajo Point

Navajo Point looks down on Escalante and Cardenas buttes and also offers a view of the Tanner Trail winding along the base of the buttes. Escalante Butte and nearby Escalante Creek were named for Francisco Escalante, a Spanish missionary who was a member of the Dominguez party. The Dominquez expedition attempted to find an overland route from Santa Fe to Monterrey on the California coast in 1776.

Cardenas Butte and nearby Cardenas Creek are named after Lieutenant Lopez de Cardenas, a member of the Coronado Expedition which traveled north from Mexico City and eventually along the present Arizona-New Mexico border. Cardenas was detached from the main expedition and sent west to confirm reports of a great river. With the assistance of Hopi guides, Cardenas reached the South Rim somewhere between Desert View and Moran Point in 1542.

Navajo Point

21.4 Desert View

Located at the east end of Desert View Drive, Desert View features the Watchtower, a structure designed by Mary Colter and inspired by the ruins of watchtowers used by prehistoric inhabitants of the canyon country. The tower and the viewpoint below it will both give you stunning views of the eastern canyon, including the especially sheer cliffs of the Palisades of the Desert and the Desert Facade.

Services at Desert View include a gift shop, snack bar, bookstore, information center, service station, campground, and restrooms. The East Entrance Station is also located at Desert View.

Kaibab National Forest- South Rim

The Tusayan Ranger District of the Kaibab National Forest encompasses the forested area south of the national park, from west of Tusayan to south of Desert View. A network of dirt forest roads crosses the national forest and provides access for recreationists, ranchers, loggers, and other users of the forest. Camping is the most popular recreational activity in the forest, and camping is allowed at Ten-X Campground on the Tusayan Ranger District as well as dispersed sites. See the Camping chapter for details.

Arizona Trail

A major section of the Arizona Trail runs through the Tusayan Ranger District. Over 800 miles long, the Arizona Trail runs north to south across Arizona from the Utah to Mexican borders. Completed in 2012, the trail is open to hikers, mountain bikers, and equestrians, except in Grand Canyon National Park where the Arizona Trail is open only to hikers.

An especially scenic portion of the Arizona Trail follows the Coconino Rim southeast from Grandview Lookout, a fire observation tower. See the Hiking chapter for information.

The Watchtower at Desert View

North Rim

From the southernmost point of this table-land the view of the canyon left the beholder solemn with the sense of awe. At high noon, under the unveiled sun, every tremendous detail leaped in glory to the sight; yet in hue and shape the change was unceasing from moment to moment. When clouds swept the heavens, vast shadows were cast; but so vast was the canyon that these shadows seemed but patches of gray and purple and umber. The dawn and the evening twilight were brooding mysteries over the dusk of the abyss; night shrouded its immensity, but did not hide it; and to none of the sons of men is it given to tell of the wonder and splendor of sunrise and sunset in the Grand Canyon of the Colorado. - Theodore Roosevelt

Vista Encantada

The North Rim and AZ 67 south of Jacob Lake are closed mid-October to mid-May. For current information, check the following web pages:

Grand Canyon National Park North Rim website:
www.nps.gov/grca/planyourvisit/directions_n_rim.htm#CP_JUMP_167594

Arizona Department of Transportation Road Conditions website:
http://www.az511.com

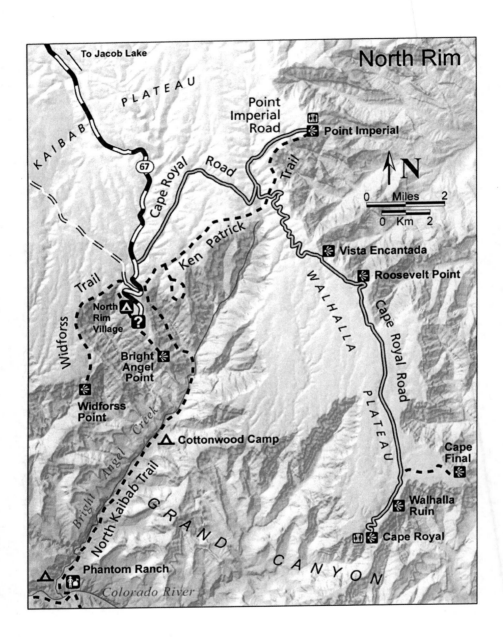

North Rim

To Jacob Lake

KAIBAB PLATEAU

67

Cape Royal Road

Point Imperial Road

Point Imperial

Trail

N

0 Miles 2
0 Km 2

Ken Patrick Trail

Vista Encantada

Roosevelt Point

WALHALLA

Cape Royal Road

Widforss Trail

North Rim Village

?

Bright Angel Point

Widforss Point

Bright Angel Creek

Cottonwood Camp

North Kaibab Trail

PLATEAU

Cape Final

Walhalla Ruin

Cape Royal

GRAND CANYON

Phantom Ranch

Colorado River

The Rim Less Visited

Because the North Rim is harder to reach than the South Rim, it gets only 10% of the park's visitors. Although it's a 21-mile hike from the South Rim to the North Rim on the Kaibab Trail, it's a five-hour, 220-mile drive on AZ 64, US 89, US 89A, and AZ 67. It's certainly worth the extra effort, however.

The Mountain Lying Down

You'll cross the nearly 10,000-foot Kaibab Plateau on the way to the North Rim. "Kaibab" is a Paiute Indian word for "mountain-lying-down". Between the gorgeous mixed coniferous forest, the alpine meadows, and the chill mountain air, you could be in Canada. In fact, you are, climate-wise. With elevations over 9,000 feet, the climate is comparable to that of southern British Columbia.

Getting Around the North Rim

There is no public transport to the North Rim, except for the Trans Canyon Shuttle (928-638-2820), which offers shuttle service between Grand Canyon Village, Marble Canyon, and North Rim Village. You'll need a car to explore the North Rim. See Getting There for more information and a list of the nearest cities with rental cars.

When to Visit

The North Rim is open from mid-May through mid-October. Though the North Rim's facilities close after mid-October, there may be limited access to the North Rim viewpoints until mid-November, depending on snowfall.

High elevation creates an alpine climate on the North Rim. Summer features cool days and chilly nights- a welcome respite from the scorching deserts below. Late summer brings almost daily afternoon thunderstorms, which create dramatic skies and spectacular sunsets. Fall weather is stable with nights below freezing and mild days, and splashes of fall color as the quaking aspen change to brilliant yellow, orange, and red. Heavy snow usually falls by November and lingers until May or June.

All of the amenities on the North Rim are located in the North Rim Village area, except for those outside the park.

North Rim Visitor Center

The North Rim Visitor Center is next to the main parking lot at Grand Canyon Lodge. Exhibits provide information on the park and the region, and there is also a bookstore.

Ranger Programs

Interpretive programs are offered during the season. Ask at the visitor center, or check the North Rim Guide, the park newspaper, for the latest information: http://www.nps.gov/grca/parknews/newspaper.htm

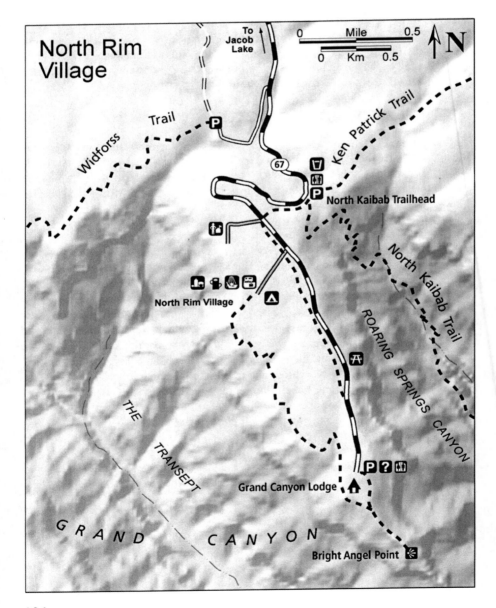

North Rim Viewpoints and Scenic Drive

Viewpoints

The view from the North Rim is quite different from that of the South Rim. Because side canyons that drain into the Colorado River from the north drain the Kaibab Plateau as well, they are much longer than their South Rim counterparts. The river is much closer to the South Rim than the north and most of the canyon's mesas, buttes, temples, and connecting ridge lines are north of the river. Summits that tend to blend in as seen from the South Rim stand out in strong relief when seen from the North Rim.

The roads to the North Rim viewpoints travel through beautiful, mixed conifer forest which is plenty of compensation for the lack of rim drives. There are also fewer viewpoints accessible by road but all of the North Rim viewpoints have unique and stunning views.

Mount Hayden from Point Imperial

Bright Angel Point

The most popular viewpoint, Bright Angel Point, is reached from the main North Rim parking lot at the end of the North Rim Road either by walking through Grand Canyon Lodge and exiting from the veranda on the left, or by skirting the lodge cabins on the left. If you walk through the lodge, you'll see why this historic park lodge is justifiably famous. Since the lodge is built in a U-shape facing the parking area, it hides the view of the canyon until you go through the main entrance and see the canyon framed by the panoramic windows of the veranda at the foot of a flight of stairs. Although perched right on the edge of the canyon, Grand Canyon Lodge is built of native stone and blends into the natural surroundings.

The view from Grand Canyon Lodge

Bright Angel Point

Whichever way you reach it, the paved trail continues about a quarter-mile along a narrow ridge to Bright Angel Point. There are a few stairs along the way. The viewpoint is within Bright Angel Canyon, a typical, long north-side canyon, so the views are more confined than other viewpoints. On the other hand, the depths of Roaring Springs Canyon are right below you, and on a quiet day you can hear Roaring Springs itself.

Point Sublime

Point Sublime is without a doubt the most stunning Grand Canyon rim viewpoint reachable by road. The turnoff is just north of the Kaibab Trailhead, on the right (west) side of the road, at the Widforss Trail Trailhead. The dirt road is 17 miles one way and is impassible until July when the last of the snow melts and the mud dries out. Even when it's dry, you'll need experience at driving back roads in remote areas as well as a high clearance, four-wheel-drive vehicle. Once there, you'll have a 300-degree view of the central Grand Canyon, including Sagittarius Ridge, Confucius and Mencius temples, the Crystal Creek area to the east, and the Shinumo Creek area and Powell Plateau to the west.

Cape Royal Scenic Drive

The Cape Royal Road is the North Rim's only paved access to rim viewpoints, but it is spectacular. It is a 23-mile one-way drive from Grand Canyon Lodge, and the suggested side trip to Point Imperial adds another 6.0 miles, for a total of 29 miles. The road passes through a beautiful mixed forest of Douglas and white firs, quaking aspen, and ponderosa pine. During the fall, the aspen lights up the forest in vibrant shades of yellow, orange, and red. The following mileage log starts from the North Rim Village parking lot at Grand Canyon Lodge and assumes you will take the side road to Point Imperial.

0.0 Grand Canyon Lodge

From the parking lot, drive north on the North Rim Road, passing North Rim Village with its campground, gas station, and general store on the left.

2.1 North Kaibab Trailhead

The only maintained trail across the Grand Canyon starts from this trailhead on the right. The North Kaibab Trail descends into Roaring Spring Canyon, and then follows Bright Angel Creek to the Colorado River, passing two backcountry campgrounds on the way. Phantom Ranch is located near the river, where hikers and mule riders can buy lunch and snacks, as well as spend the night.

3.0 Cape Royal Road

Turn right onto the Cape Royal Road (go straight ahead to exit the park.)

8.4 Point Imperial Road on the left

Point Imperial is a 3.0-mile side trip from the Cape Royal Road, which will add 6.0 miles to your drive. The mileages assume that you make this side trip, which is highly recommended.

11.4 Point Imperial

Point Imperial is the highest point on the North Rim at 8,800 feet. Here, on this lofty perch, you have a close view of Mount Hayden and a panoramic view of the complex of canyons formed by Nankoweap Creek. Nankoweap Creek has five major arms and a permanent stream in the main canyon. Hidden at the head of one of the arms is Goldwater Natural Bridge, which was discovered, lost, and then discovered again from the air by Senator Barry Goldwater. In the distance to the east and southeast, you are looking at the East Rim, which is about 3,000 feet lower than Point Imperial. The rimrock is the same on both rims– the Kaibab limestone. The reason for the difference in elevation is the East Kaibab Monocline. A monocline is a bend in the layers of rocks formed by uplift. In this case, the Kaibab Plateau, where you are standing, was uplifted 3,000 feet higher than the plateau to the east. Sometimes the rocks break along vertical fault lines, but in this case the rocks were deeply buried. Under high heat and pressure, the rocks were soft enough to bend instead of breaking. The East Kaibab Monocline is the longest exposed monocline in the world

Point Imperial

14.4 Return to Cape Royal Road

Turn left to continue the scenic drive along the Cape Royal Road.

19.0 Vista Encantada

Vista Encantada (Spanish for Enchanted View) is a small pullout on the left with picnic tables. Fir trees frame a gorgeous view of Brady Butte above the headwaters of Nankoweap Creek. It's a quiet place to have a picnic lunch and enjoy the Canyon and the rim forest. Looking to the northeast, you can see the tilted rock layers exposed on the south side of Saddle Mountain and Boundary Ridge, which form the north end of the Grand Canyon. The tilted rock layers are the result of folding along the East Kaibab Monocline.

20.6 Roosevelt Point

Roosevelt Point, a small, quiet pullout on the left, offers a view into the south arm of Nankoweap Creek as well as views across the East Rim and the Navajo Indian Reservation in the distance. Picnic tables near the parking area are a good place to take a break. An easy 0.1 mile one-way trail offers a nice, cool stroll through the North Rim forest.

26.2 Cape Final Trail

A signed trailhead marks the start of the Cape Final Trail, which leads 2.0 miles one-way to Cape Final, an east-facing promontory towering high above the headwaters of Unkar Creek. Cape Final also offers close-up views of Jupiter and Juno temples, many other Grand Canyon summits, and part of the Painted Desert and Navajo Indian Reservations in the distance to the southeast.

27.2 Walhalla Ruin

Walhalla Overlook is on the left at a large parking lot. Across the road from the viewpoint, an interpretive trail loops around a small Indian ruin. The viewpoint overlooks Unkar Creek and Unkar Delta, where the creek meets the Colorado River. An extensive pre-Columbian ruin covers the delta. Archaeological evidence shows that the inhabitants of the Unkar Delta village and the Wahalla ruin routinely traveled back and forth from rim to river, hunting in the rim forest and farming the delta with water from the Colorado River. At least one modern tribe, the Havasupai, continue this practice today, farming at Supai Village in Havasu Canyon, and raising cattle instead of hunting on the South Rim. When the first European explorers reached the Grand Canyon, the Havasupai were also farming small plots at Indian Garden on the present Bright Angel Trail.

28.1 Cliff Springs Trail

The Cliff Springs Trail starts from a small pullout on the right. It is a 0.5-mile one way trail to a rare North Rim spring. Do not drink the water without purifying it. The reason that springs and surface water are so rare on the Kaibab Plateau despite the heavy winter snowfall is the layer of porous Kaibab limestone that forms the

Roosevelt Point

Wahalla Ruin

surface of the plateau. Meltwater and rainwater promptly soaks into the ground, so that there are only a few springs and shallow lakes and no permanent streams. Additional porous layers below the Kaibab limestone let groundwater continue deep into the earth, until it encounters a layer of shale below the Redwall limestone that slows the downward percolation. The Redwall limestone is riddled with caverns dissolved out of the rock by the underground water, and some of this water finds outlets to the surface deep within the Grand Canyon. The resulting springs and permanent streams are a delight in the desert environment of the canyon.

28.7 Cape Royal

The road ends in the Cape Royal parking lot. From here it is an easy, level 0.25-mile walk to Cape Royal. This viewpoint is located at the southern tip of the Walhalla Plateau and has a 270-degree view of the eastern Grand Canyon. It is arguably the best Grand Canyon viewpoint that is accessible by paved road. Wotans Throne and Vishnu Temple, two of the most impressive of the canyon's many buttes and temples, dominate the foreground. A side trail leads out to the Angels Window overlook, which offers a view to the east at the verge of a 1,000-foot drop. Angels Window itself is a natural arch in the fin under the viewpoint.

Summits in the Grand Canyon are mountains in their own right. If Vishnu Temple was sliced off at its base and placed on the plateau, it would rise 5,000 feet above its base. Because most Grand Canyon summits are difficult to reach, requiring hours or days of strenuous cross-country hiking, the last summits weren't climbed until the 1980's. Few rockclimbers are willing to carry heavy loads of climbing and camping gear over such rough terrain to reach climbs that are on soft, dangerous rock. Even Vishnu Temple, which was first climbed in 1933 by Merrel Clubb, had only 14 ascents by 1985. Although not difficult by rockclimbing standards, climbing Vishnu Temple from the North Rim is a difficult two-day hike and scramble and the ascent of the peak requires great care.

Cape Royal

Kaibab National Forest- North Rim

The North Kaibab Ranger District of the Kaibab National Forest encompasses all of the lofty Kaibab Plateau north of the national park boundary, as well as portions of major tributary canyons of the Grand Canyon, including Kanab Creek. The national forest is managed for multiple-use and recreation coexists side-by-side with economic activities such as ranching and logging. Camping, hiking, and mountain biking are popular on the national forest.

Camping

Dispersed camping is allowed throughout the forest except where posted otherwise. There are two developed campgrounds on the North Kaibab, DeMotte Park and Jacob Lake. See the Camping chapter for more information.

Viewpoints

There are several scenic viewpoints along the east rim of the Kaibab Plateau and overlooking the Grand Canyon that are accessible via dirt forest roads. These include East Rim and Marble Canyon views, and Fire Point. You'll need a high clearance vehicle to reach these viewpoints, and to explore the many other dirt forest roads. A mountain bike is another great way to explore the forest- but be sure to bring plenty of water.

Hiking

Hikers can choose from a number of trails on the North Kaibab, including a major section of the 800-mile Arizona Trail, which crosses the Kaibab Plateau from the Utah border south to the national park boundary. Most of the Arizona Trail on the Kaibab Plateau is also open to mountain biking and equestrians. See the Hiking chapter for more information.

Wilderness

Two wilderness areas are located on the Kaibab Ranger District-Saddle Mountain and Kanab Creek wildernesses. Saddle Mountain Wilderness is on the east side of the Kaibab Plateau, just north of Boundary Ridge and Grand Canyon National Park. Kanab Creek Wilderness includes a large portion of Kanab Canyon north of the national park, and west of the Kaibab Plateau. These remote areas provide opportunities for longer hikes and backpack trips.

Toroweap

You have to get over the color green; you have to quit associating beauty with gardens and lawns; you have to get used to an inhuman scale; you have to understand geological time.
-Wallace Stegner

Lava Falls Rapids, Colorado River, near Toroweap

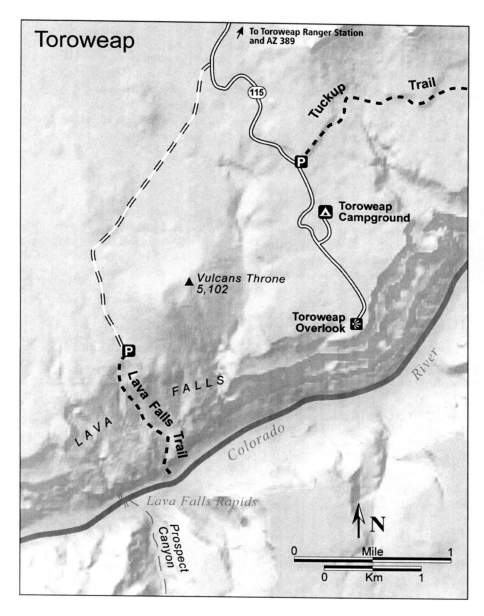

Toroweap

To Toroweap Ranger Station
and AZ 389

115

Tuckup Trail

P

Toroweap Campground

▲ Vulcans Throne
5,102

Toroweap Overlook

P

Lava Falls Trail

L A V A   F A L L S

Colorado River

Lava Falls Rapids

Prospect Canyon

N

0   Mile   1

0   Km   1

Three-thousand foot sheer red rock cliffs drop almost directly to the Colorado River at Toroweap Overlook. This is a remote part of the Grand Canyon's North Rim and is difficult to reach, but for those visitors willing to travel long dirt roads, the rewards are many. See the Getting There chapter for directions.

There are no services of any type in the Toroweap area and all visitors must bring all food, water, and other supplies with them. The portion of the access road within the park is not recommended for passenger vehicles.

Volcanoes

At Toroweap, the dramatic landscape includes nearby Vulcans Throne, an old volcanic cinder cone, which is back-dropped by the equally volcanic Uinkaret Mountains. About 500,000 years ago, these volcanoes spewed red-hot lava into the Colorado River, filling the inner gorge with steam and ultimately creating a series of lava dams 1,200 feet high and sixty miles long. These dams, which created lakes that flooded much of the Grand Canyon, have been eroded away almost without a trace by the river.

Lava Falls

Lava Falls Rapid, on the river about a mile downstream of Toroweap Overlook, is a visible and audible remnant of the catastrophic events of the geologic past. One of the hardest rapids on the river to run, the river drops thirty seven feet over and among ominous black rocks the size of small houses. The notorious rapids is not itself the remains of a lava dam, but instead formed where boulders washed down from Prospect Canyon and piled up in the Colorado River.

Toroweap Campground

This primitive campground has 11 sites and is located along the access road just before the viewpoint. Water is not available and campers must bring their own fire wood. Gathering firewood is prohibited.

Lava Falls Trail

This difficult and poorly marked trail starts near the west base of Vulcans Throne and drops 2,500 feet in 1.5 miles to the Colorado River. There are a few places where you'll have to scramble down short rock faces. Once at the river, you can hike cross-country along the river bank to Lava Falls Rapid. The south-facing slope is extremely hot in summer. Plan your hike for early morning and carry plenty of water.

Tuckup Trail

This long and meandering trail starts as an old jeep road from the Toroweap access road north of the campground and follows the Esplanade east many miles to Tuckup Canyon. Much of this old trail is faint and difficult to follow, and water sources are unreliable. The first section, starting north of the campground, is distinct and makes a good day hike.

Supai

Spring Water Dripping, land that I wandered, that place. Listen to me: forget about me, ha na. - Havasupai Farewell Song

Havasu Falls, Supai

Supai is located in Havasu Canyon, a major side canyon on the south side of the central Grand Canyon. Supai is the only settlement within the Grand Canyon and is the only post office in the United States still served by pack train. Supai is the headquarters of the Havasupai Indian Tribe, and is within the Havasupai Indian Reservation.

People of the Blue-Green Water

The Havasupai established the village at its present site hundreds of years ago, just below Havasu Spring- the source of Havasu Creek. For a couple of miles, the canyon floor is flat and the creek makes agriculture possible during the summer. Minerals dissolved in the waters of the spring tint the creek a beautiful blue-green, and in fact Havasupai means "people of the blue green water". Flowing down the lush green canyon bottom between red 1,000-foot sandstone walls, Havasu Creek makes Supai not only habitable but spectacular. But the creek isn't done yet. Below the village, the water plunges over three major waterfalls, each arguably more dramatic than the last- Havasu, Mooney, and Beaver falls.

117

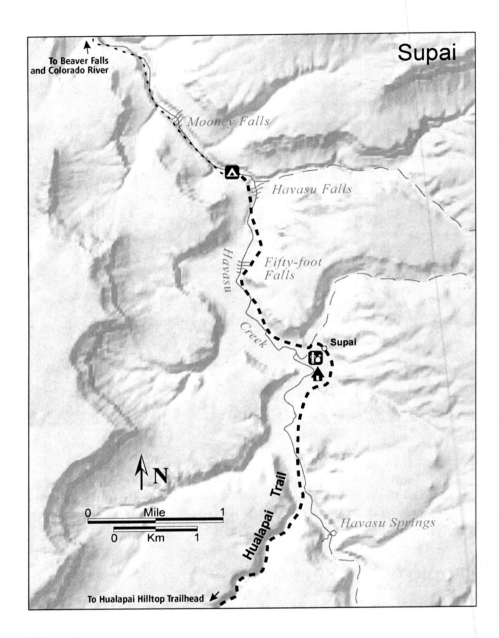

Floods

Before the floods of August 2008, there was a fourth fall, Navajo, but it was completely destroyed by a mudslide. After the flood waters receded, Navajo Falls had been bypassed by the creek, and is now dry. As compensation, two new falls were created, which are as yet unnamed. Flooding is a fact of life at Supai. Havasu Canyon

118

(known as Cataract Canyon in its upper reaches) has its headwaters more than 50 miles upstream at Bill Williams Mountain. Although the canyon is normally dry above Havasu Spring, heavy rains anywhere in Havasu Canyon's large watershed have the potential to create a flood once the waters reach the confined lower canyon.

Despite the remoteness and inherent hazards of such a remote spot, Supai has long been a popular tourist destination.

Getting to Supai

See Getting There for driving directions to Hualapai Hilltop. From this trailhead, you can get to Supai by backpacking the eight mile Hualapai Trail, hiring a Havasupai horse packer, or by helicopter.

Hiking

The most popular way to visit Supai is to hike the trail. At a minimum, this is an overnight backpack trip, but three days or more are best for exploring the canyon and falls below Supai village. Permits are required for entry and camping and can be purchased in advance from the Supai Canyon Information Center- see below. A primitive trail continues below the campground to Mooney Falls and on to the Colorado River, a distance of nine miles.

Camping

A campground accommodating up to 250 people is located along Havasu Canyon two miles below Supai village. Drinking water is provided.

Helicopter Flights

Helicopter flights are sometimes available between Hualapai Hilltop and Supai. Call Supai Canyon Information Center for reservations- see below for the phone numbers. Also, see Air Tours for other helicopter flights to Supai.

Lodging

Havasupai Lodge in Supai has twenty four rooms. Reservations must be made in advance by calling the Supai Canyon Information Center.

Havasupai Tourist Enterprises website: www.havasupai-nsn.gov/tourism.html

For more information, permits, and to make reservations for the lodge, hire a horse packer, or reserve a helicopter flight, call the Supai Canyon Information Center at 928-448-2121, 2141, 2170, or 2180.

Grand Canyon West

Skywalk at Grand Canyon West

An increasing number of visitors travel to Grand Canyon West, located on the southwest rim of the Grand Canyon on the Hualapai Indian Reservation. The Skywalk, a horseshoe-shaped glass-bottomed bridge projecting out from the rim, has made Grand Canyon West a world-famous destination which is especially popular with tour groups. Most tour groups arrive by bus or airplane. For driving directions, see Getting There.

Starting Your Tour

Grand Canyon West Tours start at the gift shop at Grand Canyon West Airport. Private cars are not allowed beyond the airport parking lot. You can buy ground tour tickets at the gift shop, and helicopter tours in the adjoining airport terminal building. Travel to the viewpoints, the Skywalk, and other attractions is by shuttle bus.

Tours

For information on Grand Canyon West, visit the Grand Canyon West website: http://grandcanyonwest.com, or call 877-716-9378 or 702-878-9378.

For air tours to Grand Canyon West from surrounding cities, see the Air Tours chapter.

Geology: Two Billion Years of Earth History

Rocks are records of events that took place at the time they formed. They are books. They have a different vocabulary, a different alphabet, but you learn how to read them. -John McPhee

Major rock layers

The Grand Canyon is a geological laboratory where much of the history of the North American continent is preserved as layers of stone exposed in the canyon walls. These rocks range in age from two billion years to several thousand years ago, representing nearly half the age of the Earth.

The rugged landforms of the Grand Canyon show that it is a geologically young feature. It is still undergoing rapid erosion, as compared to the soft, rounded forms of older geological landscapes such as the Appalachian Mountains. Current theories suggest that the canyon is five to six million years old, but that number is revised frequently in the light of new evidence.

Clearly, the Colorado River removed all of the rock eroded out of the Grand Canyon and carried it off to the Pacific Ocean, but exactly how the river carved such a complex canyon system out of the high plateaus remains the subject of conflicting theories.

Rocks: Geologic Books on a Shelf

The rocks that make up the Earth's crust are deposited as either sedimentary or igneous rocks. Either of these can be transformed by heat and pressure into metamorphic rocks. All three types of rock are exposed in the Grand Canyon.

Sedimentary Rock

Weathering and erosion of the Earth's surface, primarily by flowing water but also caused by other agents such as wind and chemical dissolution, causes rocks and soil to wear away. Streams, wind, landslides, and glaciers transport the sediment downhill to a region of deposition, usually but not always underwater. Deposition of mineral and organic particles can take place on land or underwater, causing successive strata of sediment to build up in layers. As more layers of sediment accumulate above, the lower layers are transformed into rock by heat and pressure.

Depending on the type and size of particles that are deposited, as well as the environment, different types of sedimentary rock are created. Although the technical definitions are beyond our needs here, sandstone forms when small grains of hard minerals such as quartz and feldspar are cemented together. In contrast, shale forms when the grains are silt-sized, or much finer than sand.

Limestone is usually formed underwater from skeletons of small sea creatures such as coral and mollusks. Coal is a sedimentary rock formed from accumulations of plants. Chemical precipitation of minerals in solution, as when a large lake dries up, creates sedimentary rocks from evaporite minerals such as halite (common table salt) and gypsum.

Less commonly, sedimentary rocks form from landslides, volcanic flows of hot ash, and impact debris from a meteorite strike.

Igneous Rock

Igneous rock is formed from the cooling of molten rock, or magma. Intrusive molten rock forms and solidifies underground, while extrusive rock reaches the surface in a liquid state and creates volcanic eruptions and lava flows. Magma is created from older, solid rock by heat and pressure, sometimes aided by a change in chemical composition.

Metamorphic Rock

Either sedimentary or igneous rock, as well as metamorphic rock, can be changed by the heat and pressure found deep underground into an entirely new type of rock. Although much of the original rock's character is lost during the transformation, often clues remain. Sandstone, for example, is often metamorphosed into quartzite, and shale and siltstone often become schist.

A basic prinicple of geology is that younger rocks are always deposited on top of older rocks. Study of the sequence of rock layers is our main source of knowledge about the Earth's history, including the evolution of life and changes in climate.

Simplified Geologic Cross-Section of the Grand Canyon

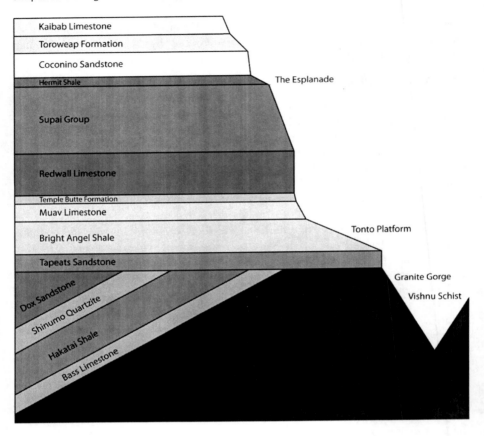

Vishnu Schist

The oldest rock formations in the canyon are found in the three deep, V-shaped, inner gorges exposed along the river bottom. Granite Gorge, the first of the three, is visible from many of the South Rim overlooks, while Middle Granite Gorge starts below the west side of Powell Plateau in the central canyon, and Lower Granite Gorge is in the Diamond Creek area in the western Grand Canyon. The Vishnu Schist is dark gray to black, and gives the three Granite Gorges their somber tone. The rocks look ancient, and they are. Originally deposited as sediments and volcanic rocks 1.9 billion years ago, the rocks were later metamorphosed into schist by the intense heat and pressures of mountain-building forces. Schist is characterized by thin layers or plates, created by extreme pressure. Liquid magma from deep in the Earth subsequently intruded into the dark schist and formed pinkish bands of granite, which can be seen zigzagging up the walls of the inner gorge like solidified lightning bolts. Erosion then wore the ancient mountains down until they formed a nearly flat plain.

Grand Canyon Supergroup

About 1.2 billion years ago, over a period of millions of years, more than 13,000 feet of sedimentary and volcanic rocks were deposited on top of the plain, which lay near a coastline and under shallow seas. The major formations in the supergroup are the Dox Limestone, Shinumo Quartzite, Hakatai Shale, and the Bass Limestone. About 725 million years ago, another round of mountain building forces lifted and tilted these layers of rock into mountain ranges. Erosion wore away at these mountains until they too were reduced to a nearly level plain with only a few remnants remaining. Today, the Grand Canyon Supergroup is exposed mainly in the far eastern Grand Canyon, where it forms the floor of the canyon as seen from Lipan Point and Desert View, and along Granite Gorge west of Bright Angel Creek. There are also outcrops of the supergroup in the Shinumo and Hakatai Canyon areas.

Tapeats Sandstone

Erosion continued for a long period when no new rocks were deposited, leaving a gap in the geologic record known as "the great unconformity." Then, about 525 million years ago, a new sea invaded the area of the Grand Canyon. Along the margins of this sea, a new layer of sediment was deposited, which eventually became the Tapeats Sandstone. It forms a distinctive, brown cliff about 200 feet high capping the Vishnu schist along the rims of Granite Gorge. Up close, you can clearly see the cross-stratified layers of coarse sand that reveal the Tapeats Sandstone's shoreline origins.

Dark gray Vishnu Schist with intrusions of lighter-colored granite form the V-shaped Granite Gorge

Tilted layers of the Grand Canyon Supergroup form the floor of the eastern Grand Canyon

Bright Angel Shale

As the ocean covering what is now the Grand Canyon region grew deeper, the sediments that were deposited became finer. Over time, thick layers of these fine sediments hardened into the Bright Angel Shale, a soft, greenish rock. Because the Bright Angel Shale is thickest in the eastern Grand Canyon, it erodes out into a plateau known as the Tonto Platform. The Tonto Platform is prominent from South Rim viewpoints from Moran Point to Pima Point. The Tonto Trail takes advantage of the relatively easy terrain to wind along the Tonto Platform for more than 70 miles.

Muav Limestone

Toward the top of the Bright Angel Shale, gray layers of Muav Limestone begin to interfinger with the shale, showing that the ancient ocean was continuing to deepen around 505 million years ago. The sea receded and advanced several times during this period, resulting in the small cliffs of gray Muav Limestone now exposed toward the top of the Bright Angel Shale slopes.

Redwall Limestone

By 340 million years ago, deep ocean covered the entire Grand Canyon region. As trillions of microscopic sea creatures lived and died, their tiny shells rained down on the ocean floor, forming layers of sediment that eventually formed the Redwall Limestone. Today, the Redwall Limestone forms a 550-foot cliff that persists

Thick layers of Bright Angel Shale erode into the Tonto Platform

The hikers are camping on ledges of Tapeats Sandstone. Above, the broad slope is formed on the Bright Angel Shale. A small cliff of greenish Muav Limestone is visible on the left, and above it, the massive Redwall Limestone cliff.

throughout the length of the Grand Canyon, snaking in and out of side canyons to form hundreds of miles of Redwall rim. Fresh exposures of Redwall Limestone are pearly gray, but the massive cliffs are stained deep red by runoff from the overlying rocks.

All the cliffs in the Grand Canyon present challenges to would-be explorers, but the Redwall is the most formidable. Within the Grand Canyon, there are only about two hundred known natural routes though the Redwall. Most current Grand Canyon trails, including the Bright Angel Trail, take advantage of such natural breaks, but the Kaibab Trail is an engineered route that required plenty of explosives to create. It was probably the Redwall Limestone that stopped the Spanish conquistadors from reaching the Colorado River in 1540.

Supai Group

After such a long period under the Redwall sea, the region was once again exposed as dry land, and a period of erosion left stream channels filled with river sediments on the top of the Redwall Limestone. Around 315 million years ago, a sea began encroaching on the area once again. This resulted in the deposition of the red rocks of the Supai Group, alternating layers of sandstone, shale, and limestone. The harder layers of limestone and sandstone form cliffs, with some, like the uppermost layer known as the Esplanade Sandstone, up to 200 feet high. The layers of soft shale form slopes between the cliffs.

Hermit Shale

About 280 million years ago, a long period of tidal flat deposition resulted in the Hermit Shale, a bright red formation that forms slopes at the top of the Supai Group. In the eastern canyon, along the Desert Facade, the Hermit Shale disappears and the Coconino Sandstone above forms sheer cliffs overlying the Supai Group below. In the area visible from Moran Point to Hermits Rest, the Hermit Shale forms the deep red slopes at the base of the Coconino Sandstone buttes and temples. In the western canyon, the Hermit Shale increases to more than 1,500 feet thick. Here, the Esplanade, a broad terrace, forms in the Hermit Shale, replacing the Tonto Platform as the dominant mid-level terrace in the Grand Canyon.

The South Kaibab Trail descending through the upper Supai Group

The Coconino Sandstone is the lowest white cliff. The Toroweap formation is the slope above, and the Kaibab Limestone forms the rim cliffs.

Coconino Sandstone

More erosion planed off the upper surface of much of the Hermit Shale then a vast, Sahara-like desert of giant sand dunes covered the region by around 275 million years ago. This resulted in the formation of the 350-foot thick Coconino Sandstone. The sloping faces of the ancient dunes are clearly visible in the cross-stratified layers. If examined with a good hand lens, the sand grains that make up the Coconino Sandstone are clearly sandblasted, an effect created by wind tumbling the sand grains together. From the rim viewpoints the Coconino Sandstone is the prominent buff-colored to white cliff about 1,000 feet below the rim.

The Kaibab Limestone forms the rim cap rock throughout most of the Grand Canyon. The slope at the lower left is the top of the Toroweap Formation.

Toroweap Formation

Around 273 million years ago, changing near-shore ocean environments caused the deposition of the shale, limestone, and sandstone layers of the Toroweap Formation. These pale yellow and gray layers form steep slopes and small cliffs directly below the rim cliffs.

Kaibab Limestone

An off-white to cream-colored cliff about 250 feet high forms nearly all of the rim of the Grand Canyon and much of the surface of the plateaus on either side of the canyon. This layer, the Kaibab Limestone, was deposited in an ocean about 270 million years ago. Fossil seashells are found throughout the Kaibab Limestone and can be seen in the rocks along the Rim Trail.

The Missing Rocks

As much as 20,000 feet of younger rocks once covered the Grand Canyon region, but have been entirely eroded away except for isolated remnants at Cedar Mountain and Red Butte near the South Rim. These younger rocks still cover large areas of northeastern Arizona, east of the Grand Canyon.

Volcanoes

On the western portion of the North Rim, volcanic activity began about six million years ago and continued until several thousand years ago, resulting in lava flows on the Shivwits Plateau and cinder cones in the Uinkaret Mountains and at Vulcans Throne near Toroweap. Lava flows dammed the Colorado River at least four times, creating dams as much as 1,200 feet high and 50 miles thick along the course of the river. The lakes behind these lava dams would have backed up all the way to Lees Ferry. As a perfect illustration of the power of the Colorado River, each of these massive rock dams have been eroded away, leaving only a few patches of lava rock on the lower walls of the Canyon to prove they existed.

The River That Flowed Uphill

There's little doubt that the Colorado River carved the Grand Canyon. But exactly how it did so is still a mystery. Water flows downhill, so when a river encounters rising terrain it is diverted, always seeking the path of least resistance to reach the sea.

So why does the course of the Colorado River cut through the Kaibab and Coconino plateaus almost at their highest point? As the broader Colorado Plateau rose, lifted by the same mountain-building forces that raised the Rocky Mountains, the Colorado River should have gone somewhere else.

One current theory suggests that the present Colorado River achieved its course by a combination of headward erosion and stream capture. Because water rushing down the steep slopes at the upper ends of the canyons has far more erosive power than the gentler flows in the lower canyons, erosion proceeds rapidly headward into the surrounding plateau.

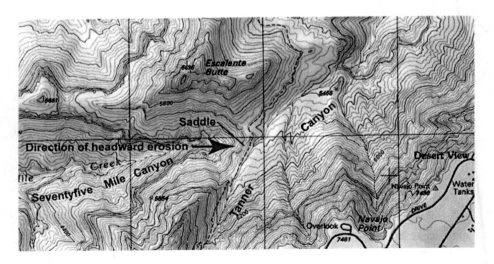

At the center of this map, Seventyfive Mile Canyon, on the left, is about to capture Tanner Canyon, on the right.

Looking across Tanner Canyon to the saddle at the head of Seventyfive Mile Canyon, seen just below and right of photo center

If the headward-eroding canyon rim encounters another, lower-gradient stream that can't deepen its bed as rapidly, it will capture and divert the headwaters of the lower-gradient stream, further increasing the runoff and erosion in the steeper canyon.

This process can be seen today in the eastern Grand Canyon where Seventyfive Mile Canyon is eroding away the saddle at its head. Very soon, geologically speaking, Seventyfive Mile Canyon will capture the drainage of Tanner Canyon, which is only a few dozen yards from the saddle, and divert upper Tanner Canyon into Seventyfile mile Canyon.

According to the stream capture theory, around 70 million years ago what is now the upper Colorado River east of the Grand Canyon actually flowed in the opposite direction, fed by the Little Colorado River. The Little Colorado drained mountain highlands in eastern Arizona, ultimately draining into an inland lake in the vicinity of the present Rocky Mountains.

About 16 million years ago, the basin-and-range country of far western Arizona formed, causing drainage to increase from the rising plateaus in the Grand Canyon region. This caused the ancestral lower Colorado River to erode headward to the east, ultimately capturing the upper Colorado River in the vicinity of the present confluence of the Little Colorado and Colorado rivers.

At the same time, the rise of the Rocky Mountains disrupted the northeast flow of the Colorado River and eventually caused the river to reverse its flow. The Colorado River now flows southwest through ever deeper Marble Canyon, which is carved directly up the slope of the surrounding Marble Plateau. All the side canyons meet the river angling upstream. From the air or on a small-scale map, the effect is striking; the Colorado River is flowing the wrong way.

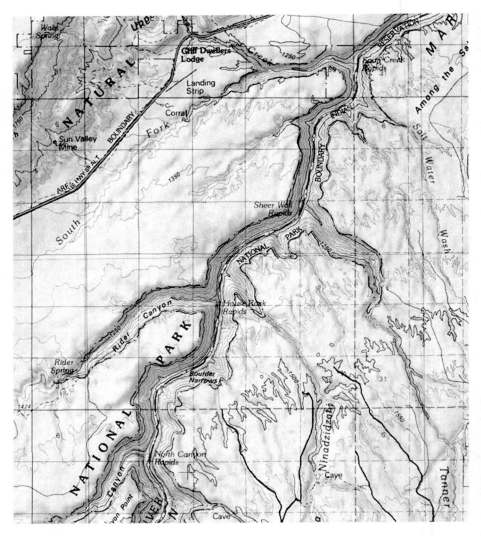

Backward tributaries in Marble Canyon

The modern course of the Colorado River was established by about two to six million years ago. Since then, successive glacial periods followed by melting repeatedly sent large volumes of water down the Colorado River and its main tributary, Green River, rapidly increasing its depth. Some geologists think the depth of the Grand Canyon was doubled in this way during the last two million years.

Grand Canyon Today

Geologically, the Grand Canyon extends from Lees Ferry at the foot of the Echo Cliffs 277 river miles downstream to the Grand Wash Cliffs. Although the character of the Grand Canyon changes along its length, many of the same rock layers are present along the entire distance, notably the Kaibab Limestone, the Supai Formation, and the Redwall Limestone.

Marble Canyon

The rock layers that form the walls of the Grand Canyon are first exposed at Lees Ferry. Here, Glen Canyon ends abruptly and the Colorado River flows between low banks for a short distance. Once the site of a ferry and a ranch operated by John D. Lee, Lees Ferry is the only point along the river above the Grand Canyon that is accessible by road. Just below the boat ramp, the river starts to cut into Marble Plateau, forming Marble Canyon. Where the river flows under Navajo Bridge (the replacement for the ferry), Marble Canyon is already 800 feet wide and 400 feet deep. Marble Canyon differs from Grand Canyon in that it is a single main canyon with tributary canyons, and the rims are close above the river. As the Colorado River flows southwest, the plateau rises. When Marble Canyon ends at Boundary Ridge, it is 4,000 feet deep and two miles wide.

Grand Canyon

As the Colorado River enters Grand Canyon, the river canyon widens to more than eight miles. Instead of a single, narrow canyon, the Grand Canyon is a complex maze of side canyons, mesas, and buttes. The heads of the major side canyons cut into the rims, forming cliff-bound amphitheaters. The ridges between the side canyons are carved into large mesas, isolated buttes, and towering pinnacles. From the rim viewpoints or from the air, it is obvious that the Grand Canyon is a single canyon system. Down in the canyon, however, along the river or hiking, the rims are partially or completely hidden so it appears as if you're deep in the heart of a mountain range.

Desert Facade

As the river continues south through the eastern Grand Canyon, it flows through a canyon floored by the soft rocks of the Bright Angel Shale, and the river banks are relatively accessible. The 550-foot Redwall Limestone cliffs tower above the river. Major side canyons enter mainly from the west, as the river flows close to the east rim. Known as the Desert Facade, the especially steep ramparts below the east rim are a result of a missing rock layer, the Hermit Shale, which causes the near-vertical Coconino Sandstone cliff to rest directly on the cliff-forming Esplanade Sandstone.

Palisades of the Desert

As the Colorado River reaches the confluence with the Little Colorado River, the Tapeats Sandstone emerges at river level and forms an inner gorge about 200 feet deep, making the river nearly inaccessible. Towering, cliff-bound summits such as

Marble Canyon

One of many Grand Canyon summits, distant Vishnu Temple rises higher than the South Rim

The steep buttresses of the distant Desert Facade, center rim, and Palisades of the Desert, right rim, are caused by a relative absence of the soft layers of shale that form terraces between the Kaibab Limestone, the Coconino Sandstone, and the Supai Group further west in the canyon

Chuar Butte on the west face the equally imposing Palisades of the Desert across the river on the east.

Grand Canyon Supergroup

Below Desert View, the river changes course from south to west, and the colorful, tilted layers of the Grand Canyon Supergroup form the floor of the canyon. Desert View, Lipan Point, and Cape Royal are good vantage points for observing the relatively open terrain eroded from the soft shale members of the supergroup. The Colorado River is also readily visible. From a distance, the terrain near the river looks gentle, but only in contrast with the towering cliffs above. It is still very difficult, rough terrain for the hiker.

Granite Gorge

Below Moran Point, the Colorado River enters Granite Gorge, as the Grand Canyon Supergroup disappears and the Vishnu Schist is exposed. The V-shaped gorge rises rapidly to 1,500 feet deep, rimmed by the brown Tapeats Sandstone. Access to the river from above is nearly impossible, except down the few side canyons that are not blocked by dry falls or other obstacles. Landing places for river rafts are scarce and the rapids are especially fierce. In fact, five of the hardest ten rapids in the Grand Canyon are found along Granite Gorge.

Rapids

All of the rapids on the Colorado River in the Grand Canyon are formed by debris washed down tributary canyons into the river. Because the tributaries have a steeper gradient than the river, the tributaries are capable of moving larger rocks. Rapids are

Monument Rapid was formed by debris washed down Monument Creek

formed when floods in the side canyons cause debris flows to reach the river, partially damming it. The Colorado River, using its load of sand like a giant rasp, gradually wears away the rocks in the rapid. If no new floods occur in a given tributary, the rapid at its foot will eventually disappear completely. Before the construction of Glen Canyon Dam upstream, periodic floods on the Colorado River frequently modified rapids in the Grand Canyon.

Crystal Rapid, formed by debris from Slate Canyon on the south side, and Crystal Creek on the north side, was an unremarkable rapid until December 1966. During a winter storm, several inches of rain fell on snowpack in the Crystal Creek drainage, causing a major flood and debris flow along Crystal Creek. Overnight, Crystal Rapid became one of the most difficult rapids in the Grand Canyon. Since then, the power of floods to modify rapids on the Colorado River has been demonstrated during the artificial floods released from Glen Canyon Dam in 1983 and 1996. Both of these engineered floods changed the character of Crystal Rapid.

Tonto Platform

As the Colorado River flows under the two suspension bridges at the mouth of Bright Angel Creek, the site of Phantom Ranch and the crossing point of the trans-canyon Kaibab Trail, Granite Gorge is at its awesome best. The rim viewpoints from Yaki Point to Hermits Rest offer only occasional glimpses of the river, mostly hidden in its steep-sided inner gorge. In this portion of the Grand Canyon, the soft Bright Angel Shale erodes into a broad terrace, the Tonto Platform, about 4,000 feet below the rim.

Side Canyons

Major side canyons branch north and south from Granite Gorge. Because the river cut through the surrounding plateau south of its highest point, the plateaus beyond the both rims drain to the south. This means that precipitation falling on the South Rim flows away from the canyon, while precipitation falling on the North Rim flows into the canyon. The extra flow makes the north-side canyons longer, so that in the section of the canyon between Moran Point and Hermits Rest the river is much closer to the South Rim than the north. The terrain on the north side of the river is more complex than it is on the south side and most of the major buttes and summits are on the north side of the river. From the South Rim viewpoints, the North Rim is partially obscured by the mesas and buttes rising nearly as high as the rim. From the North Rim, the relief north of the river is more apparent and the South Rim appears to be a monolithic wall.

The Esplanade

About 20 miles west of Grand Canyon Village, the Bright Angel Shale thins to the point that the Tonto Platform tapers away. Meanwhile, the Hermit Shale has become much thicker, so a new terrace, the Esplanade, forms on the top of the Supai Group about 2,000 feet below the rim. The Esplanade becomes broader to the west as the Hermit Shale thickens and is the dominant terrace in the central and western Grand Canyon. Like the Tonto Platform, the Esplanade is also drained by major side canyons and their tributaries.

The Esplanade

Temple Butte Limestone

A new formation appears in the western Grand Canyon- the Temple Butte Limestone. Found only in a few places in the eastern Grand Canyon, the Temple Butte Limestone thickens and becomes a major cliff-forming layer in the western canyon. The Temple Butte Limestone forms the lower cliffs below Toroweap Overlook and helps make the 3,000-foot inner gorge at Toroweap so dramatic.

At Grand Canyon West, the Temple Butte Limestone is much thicker than the overlying Redwall Limestone, and together the two formations form a steep series of cliffs nearly 3,000 feet high. In this area, the Redwall Limestone generally forms the South Rim because the Supai Group and the rocks above have been eroded away. Across the river from Grand Canyon West, the higher North Rim is still formed from the Kaibab Limestone, and the Esplanade is present, carved from the Hermit Shale. The Shivwits Plateau forms the westernmost part of the North Rim, and this extremely isolated area is often capped by lava flows.

Grand Wash Cliffs

The Grand Canyon ends abruptly about ten miles west of Grand Canyon West, at the Grand Wash Cliffs. This west-facing, 4,000-foot line of cliffs also marks the western edge of the Colorado Plateau. The effect is dramatic- the Colorado River suddenly emerges from the Grand Canyon into gently rolling desert hills. When it is full, Lake Mead, the reservoir created by Hoover Dam, floods the lower Grand Canyon below Separation Canyon. As the Colorado River gradually merges with the still waters of the lake, the river drops its load of sediment, silting in the rapids and creating high silt banks along the river and the lower side canyons. When Lake Mead is low, the river current resumes, but lacks the power to excavate the rapids. The result is that there are no rapids on the Colorado River in the area of Grand Canyon West.

Plants and Animals: Home is the Grand Canyon

Has joy any survival value in the operations of evolution? I suspect that it does; I suspect that the morose and fearful are doomed to quick extinction. Where there is no joy there can be no courage; and without courage all other virtues are useless. -Edward Abbey

Spring flower on the Tonto Platform

Grand Canyon is a home- home for many species of plants and animals, some common, some found nowhere else. Standing in the rim forests, it is easy to look down at the canyon and think of it as totally barren. Most of the canyon is a desert, it's true, but that desert actually teems with life, much of it especially adapted to survive the harsh climate. And because the Grand Canyon encompasses a wide range of elevations, home can be a burrow under a rock in the scorching hot Granite Gorge, or a nest high in a Douglas fir on the lofty Kaibab Plateau.

Water, the Key to Life

As everywhere else on our planet, the key to survival is water. And there is water in the Grand Canyon, aside from the obvious abundance of the Colorado River itself.

144

Waterpockets on the Esplanade

Springs

Moisture that falls on the high plateaus surrounding the canyon mostly soaks deep into the ground, traveling downward through the porous layers of sandstone and limestone until it reaches impervious layers of shale. Unable to sink deeper, the groundwater forms a massive water table several thousand feet below the surface of the plateau. All this groundwater has carved channels through the Redwall Limestone. Some of these underground rivers suddenly and dramatically express themselves as huge springs bursting out of caves in the Redwall Limestone at places such as Roaring Springs, Thunder Spring, Tapeats Spring, and Deer Spring. Other springs aren't so dramatic, but even the smallest seep spring is an oasis for life.

Permanent Streams

Because of the springs, there are a surprising number of permanent creeks in the Grand Canyon, especially on the north side of the river- Nankoweap Creek, Kwagunt Creek, Lava Creek, Clear Creek, and Bright Angel Creek, to name a few.

Water Pockets

Water pockets form where large expanses of bare sandstone collect rain and snow-melt into shallow pools on the bare rock. Over time, the water's chemical action dissolves the calcite cement holding the sand grains together, and when the pockets are dry, wind carries the loose sand away, deepening the pocket. Some water pockets are huge, holding hundreds of gallons of water and lasting well into the summer or even all year. Others dry up within hours or days of the rainfall. Water pockets are an essential source of water for wildlife, and hikers also depend on them in many parts of the Grand Canyon.

145

Clear Creek

Desert River

Unlike rivers in gentler regions, the Colorado River is only a boon to the life actually living in the water, and on the river's immediate banks. Confined by steep canyon walls, the river can't spread out during floods, which would normally deposit rich soil over a valley bottom. Even the river's groundwater is kept from spreading out by the rock channel.

Life Zones and Plant Communities

Plants and animals tend to form interdependent and distinct communities in their particular climate. Because the range of elevation in the Grand Canyon region is so great, 7,500 feet, there are five distinct lifezones in the Grand Canyon. These are marked by indicator plants typical of each lifezone. Nature is rarely as simple as it seems, and so it is with lifezones. Each lifezone merges gradually with the one above, and the lifezones occur higher or lower on south and north facing slopes, but still the lifezone concept is useful to understand how wild communities relate to their environment.

Riparian Life Zone

Along the Colorado River, the permanent streams, and the more reliable springs, riparian (streamside) plants and animals find a home. Arroweed, catclaw acacia, western honey mesquite, and several willows are common native plants. Tamarisk and camel thorn, non-native introduced plants, thrive in the riparian zone and form dense thickets. The Colorado River and its permanent tributary streams support native fish. In fact, tributary streams are often the last refuge of native fish driven out of the main river by the changes brought by the construction of Glen Canyon Dam upstream of the Grand Canyon. If there is enough water and floods don't disrupt their growth, large cottonwood trees take root. Seeps and springs create small riparian zones that harbor plants such as maidenhair fern and redbud trees.

Mohave and Great Basin Desert Life Zones

Away from the Colorado River, at the lowest elevations of the Grand Canyon, are the desert communities- Mohave Desert in the western Grand Canyon, and Great Basin Desert in the eastern canyon, where the lowest elevations are 1,500 feet higher. Typical plants are creosote, white bursage, brittlebrush, western honey mesquite, four-wing saltbush, rabbitbrush, blackbrush, and big sagebrush.

Pinyon-Juniper

At intermediate elevations, pinyon pines and juniper trees grow in an open woodland commonly referred to as pinyon-juniper. One-seed juniper grows about 10 to 15 feet high, and single leaf pinyon pine, which favors slightly moister slopes, grows 15 to 30 feet tall. In the open spaces between the little trees, Mormon tea, Utah agave, narrowleaf yucca, winterfat, dropseed, bananna yucca, needlegrass, snakeweed, Indian ricegrass, and big sagebrush are common.

Transition Life Zone

At the highest Grand Canyon elevations, on protected north-facing slopes, and on both rims,100-foot tall ponderosa pines create an open, park-like forest. Gambel oak, which is deciduous, and Arizona white oak, which is evergreen, are common, as is fescue, mountain mahogany, manzanita, elderberry, and creeping mahonia.

Canadian Life Zone

On the Kaibab Plateau and on north-facing terraces just below the rims, an alpine forest typical of southern British Columbia contains a beautiful mix of ponderosa pine, Douglas fir, white fir, Colorado blue spruce, Englemann spruce, mountain ash, and quaking aspen. Cinquefoils, asters, lupines, grasses, groundsels, yarrow, and asters grow on the forest floor during the short summers.

On the highest parts of the Kaibab Plateau, at nearly 9,000 feet, big galleta, Indian ricegrass, three awns, and blue and black gramma grasses cover expansive alpine meadows such as DeMotte Park.

Plants of the Grand Canyon

Cactus

Cactus have spines instead of leaves and have green, fleshy stems which both conserve water and carry out food production. They are are highly evolved to handle the desert environment, but many species have little tolerance for cold. In the canyon, that limits cactus to the smaller species like desert prickly pear, which is common on the Tonto Platform. Other cactus include California barrel, whipple cholla, beavertail, claret cup, fishhook, and Englemann hedgehog. Claret cup blooms with a stunning red flower after wet winters.

Grasses

Side oats, blue and black gramma, Indian ricegrass, and big galleta are among the native grasses found in the canyon. Exotics, or introduced grasses, include Kentucky bluegrass, red and smooth brome, and cheatgrass. Exotics often compete with native grasses. Cheatgrass is especially difficult because it greatly increases the fire danger once it cures during the summer.

Ferns

Ferns favor moist sites such as crevices, ledges, and boulder piles. Maidenhair and brittle fern prefer springs and seeps. All ferns reproduce from spores rather than flowers.

Hedgehog cactus

Freshwater Plants

Springs support miniature gardens of columbine, horsetail, watercress, monkeyflower, and rushes. The Colorado River not only supports a narrow but important riparian life zone, the river itself contains green algae, which small aquatic animals depend on for food.

Lichens

Lichens are common in the Grand Canyon because of the vast amount of exposed rock. Lichens are tiny communities of two or more plants such as a green algae and a fungus. The fungus extracts nutrients from the rock and protects the algae from the harsh environment. In turn, the green algae uses sunlight to produce food by photosynthesis. Lichens are most common on the north sides of rocks where the temperature is lower. Lichens store water during storms and can store more than their weight in water.

Wildflowers

When conditions are favorable, the spring wildflower displays in the canyons have to be seen to be believed. A wet winter and early spring followed by warming temperatures appear to create ideal conditions. Red and orange flowers include globemallow, Indian paintbrush, penstemon, skyrocket, red columbine, and crimson monkeyflower. Yellow flowers are common and hard to identify but some examples are groundcherry, broom snakeweed, Hookers primrose, ragweed, and common mullein. White flowers include sacred datura, evening primrose, tidy fleabane, desert tobacco, yarrow, baby white aster, white violet, and watercress. Pink and purple flowers include Rocky Mountain bee plant, Rocky Mountain iris, Grand Canyon phacelia, toadflax penstemon, and Palmer lupine.

Indian paintbrush

Animals of the Grand Canyon

Amphibians

Great Basin spadefoot toad and Utah tiger salamander are common in the rim forests. The desert canyons don't seem to be the kind of place you'd expect amphibians, but the permanent tributaries and the Colorado River support red-spotted toads, Woodhouse's Rocky Mountain toad, and canyon treefrogs.

Fish

Non-native fish such as carp and trout dominate the Colorado River because of the artificial cold temperature of the water released from Glen Canyon Dam upstream of the Grand Canyon. These introduced exotics have driven the native squawfish, bonytail chub, and roundtail chub to extinction. Other native fish survive in the warm tributaries such as the Little Colorado River. These include flannelmouth sucker, speckled dace, and bluehead sucker. Surviving but endangered species include razorback sucker and humpback chub.

Insects and Spiders

Common insects of the coniferous forests and desert scrub include wasps, tarantula hawks, honey bees, stink bugs, black flies, beetles, black ants, and butterflies. Scorpions thrive in the lower deserts, while garden spiders, solpugids, wood spiders, black widow spiders, and tarantulas prefer the forests. Insects are common along the permanent streams and the Colorado River, including butterflies, black flies, mayflies, stone flies, beetles, moths, and fire ants. Giant hairy desert scorpions and bark scorpions are also common.

Mammals

Desert bighorn sheep, thriving now that the competing feral burros have been removed, are a common sight, often in small bands moving along ledges. Coyotes, with their distinctive twilight song, are common, especially near water, as are ringtail cats and spotted skunks. Mule deer are common on both rims and throughout the canyon. Neatly clipped willows along streams are signs of beaver. Bats can be seen in the evening twilight as they dart after insects. Raccoons, mountain lions, bobcats, weasels, and gray foxes are rarer.

Woodrat middens are common in the desert scrub. These rodents live in well-protected burrows under boulders and overhangs, and bring twigs, cactus spines, and almost anything else that is loose, creating middens that may be used for many generations. Study of the midden contents often reveals details of past climate and vegetation patterns in the Grand Canyon.

In the rim forests, shrews, mule deer, black bear, elk, porcupines, red squirrels, and tassel-eared squirrels are all common. Black bear are generally shy of people and rarely seen.

Two distinct species of tassel-eared squirrels have evolved on each rim, separated by the desert gulf they cannot cross. The two species were once a single species but drier, warmer weather after the last glacial period caused the forests to retreat to the highest part of the plateaus, and created the present desert environment in the Grand Canyon. As a result, the Abert squirrel, gray with white underparts, is found today on the South Rim and other ponderosa pine forests in Arizona, while the Kaibab squirrel, with its black belly and white tail, is found only on the Kaibab Plateau. Both squirrels have upright tassels on their ears and large fluffy tails. Tassel-eared squirrels are completely dependent on the ponderosa pine for their survival. They can often be seen running along the ground to the nearest tree or sitting high on a branch scolding at intruders.

Bobcats

Reptiles

Reptiles inhabit most of the canyon below the rims but are more common near water, where their prey, small rodents, insects, and vegetation, is concentrated. There are many small lizards and two larges ones, the chuckwalla, and the Gila monster, which is over a foot long. Non-poisonous king snakes, gopher snakes, and racers are fairly common. Four species of poisonous rattlesnakes are found in the Grand Canyon- the Hopi, Great Basin, Mojave, and Grand Canyon pink rattlesnakes. All rattlesnakes are pit vipers and sense their prey through ground vibration and infrared (heat). Due to lack of water, reptiles are not as common in the rim forests, but you may see the mountain short-horned lizard.

Gray fox

Birds

Birds mostly favor the Colorado River riparian zone, and many are winter visitors, such as the bald eagle. Peregrine falcons nest on the cliffs of the inner gorges, and feed on the smaller birds and bats that are found near the river. Birds are not as common away from water, in the desert scrub and pinyon-juniper woodland. Two exceptions are the pinyon jay, which has a distinctive quiet, high-pitched, quavering caw, and the canyon wren, which has a melodic descending trill that echoes through the side canyon it calls home.

California condors, the largest North American land bird, were once native to northern Arizona and were reintroduced to the Grand Canyon region in 1996 as part of a plan to save them from extinction. They are now a common sight as they soar over the rim viewpoints, and their nearly 10 foot wingspan and triangular white patches on the underside of their wings makes them unmistakable.

Mountain lion

People and the Canyon

The region is of course, altogether valueless. It can be approached only from the South, and after entering it there is nothing to do but leave. Ours has been the first, and will doubtless be the last, party of whites to visit this profitless locality. It seems intended by nature that the Colorado River, along with the greater portion of its lonely and majestic way, shall be forever unvisited and undisturbed. -Lt. Joseph Ives

Hiker on the Esplanade

The Grand Canyon has always had a powerful effect on humans, as evidenced by the reverence with which it is regarded by both ancient and modern people. Through art ranging from split twig figurines woven from a single piece of willow wood, to paintings and photography, humans have attempted to express the feelings evoked by the Grand Canyon.

Natives

There is evidence that native peoples lived in the Grand Canyon region for more than 12,000 years. Ruins and artifacts show that people lived in and utilized the resources of the Grand Canyon until about 800 years ago. Then, the population of the canyon crashed abruptly and dwellings were abandoned. At present, the only people living within the Grand Canyon are the Havasupai, but tribes living on the plateaus above, including the Hualapai, Mohave, southern Paiutes, Navajo, and Hopi, have also long made use of the canyon's resources.

The Spanish

Spanish conquistadors led by the explorer Cardenas were the first party of Europeans to see the Grand Canyon. Detached from the main body of the Coronado Expedition, the Cardenas party reached the South Rim somewhere between Lipan Point and Moran Point in 1540. Although their Hopi guides almost certainly knew of routes to the river, they weren't telling, and the Spanish searched in vain for ten days before giving up. Still, just reaching the Grand Canyon across the dry and dangerous deserts was a major accomplishment less than 50 years after Columbus first reached the New World.

More than two hundred years would pass before the next Spanish party saw the Grand Canyon. Traveling alone, Father Garces approached the canyon from the lower Colorado River in 1776. He befriended the local Indians who clearly gave him good advice, because he was guided to the village of Supai and then made his way along the South Rim in the area of Grandview Point.

Trappers

During the 1820's, a fur trapper, James Pattie, and his party made their way from Black Canyon on the Colorado River, along the North Rim, and on to the Zuni villages in New Mexico. Pattie published his adventures as a Personal Narrative, which was part fact and part fiction. Other fur trappers undoubtedly visited the Grand Canyon to trap beaver on its streams, but if so they left no record.

Americans

After the Mexican-American War of 1848, the United States acquired the southwestern portion of North America north of the Gila River and energetically started to explore the hostile deserts of the region. A flood of gold seekers and emigrants sought routes to the California gold fields in 1849, and soon a wagon road was established across the Coconino Plateau south of the Grand Canyon. But the course of the Colorado River, and the Grand Canyon itself, was still a mystery.

Lt. Joseph Ives

In 1857, Army Lieutenant Joseph Ives was sent up the lower Colorado River in a steamboat to find the head of navigation. After wrecking on a rock in Black Canyon below the present site of Hoover Dam, Lieutenant Ives continued overland. He descended Peach Springs Wash to the Colorado River and visited Supai. Members of his party included John Newberry, the first geologist to study the Grand Canyon, and Bavarian artist and cartographer Baron Friedrich von Egloffstein, who produced the first detailed maps of a portion of the Grand Canyon. But the Grand Canyon still didn't even have a name, usually being referred to as the "big canyon." And all of these early visitors regarded the Grand Canyon with horror, as a useless place with a completely inaccessible river.

Powell's River Expeditions

During 1869-71, Major John Wesley Powell, a geologist and one-armed American Civil War veteran, led two expeditions down the Green and Colorado River systems. He also explored the plateaus surrounding the canyon and studied the local Indian tribes. He literally put the canyon on the map, naming it "The Grand Canyon of the Colorado." He published both professional papers on the canyon as well as a popular account of his journeys. His and the accounts of other members of his parties helped to popularize the Grand Canyon.

Stanton's River Expedition

Robert Brewster Stanton led an expedition through the Grand Canyon in 1889-90 to survey it for a river-level railroad. Several accidents, including the loss of the company president by drowning early on the first attempt to run the river (for some reason Stanton did not include life jackets on the trip), and difficulties getting financing, doomed the proposed railroad. But Stanton did have one effect- he wrote a book about his adventures in the Grand Canyon that popularized river running.

Miners

Attracted by the large expanses of rock open to exploration, prospectors and miners began to explore the canyon. In the 1880's, William Wallace Bass came to the Grand Canyon from the east coast for his health, and the dry air worked it's magic. He raised a family at Bass Camp on the South Rim to the west of the present village, built the Bass Trail, the first trail across the canyon, and developed copper mines on both sides of the river. At about the same time, Pete Berry developed the Tanner and Grandview trails in the eastern Grand Canyon. Berry's Last Chance Mine on Horseshoe Mesa was one of the few Grand Canyon mines to show a profit, if only for a short time. John Hance built trails down Red and Hance canyons to reach asbestos deposits on the north side of the river. Fibers from his mines were used in fireproof theater curtains as far away as Europe.

Tourism

Before long, increasing numbers of people were coming to the Grand Canyon to see it, not to exploit it. The miners quickly found that guiding these dudes was far more profitable than mining. The first rim hotel was soon built near Grandview Point, and Hance built rustic accommodations for his clients at the mouth of Red Canyon on the Colorado River. Bass guided tourists on his Bass Trail to the North Rim, crossing the river on a ferry at low water and on a tram cable at high water.

The Railroad

In 1901, the Santa Fe Railroad completed a spur track from Williams to the present Grand Canyon Village area on the South Rim, replacing the arduous all-day stage trip from Flagstaff with a short, comfortable train ride. Grand Canyon Village quickly developed as the new focal point of Grand Canyon tourism, replacing Bass Camp to

Grand Canyon Railway arriving at the South Rim

the west and Grandview Hotel to the east. To accommodate the increasing flood of visitors, the railroad completed the El Tovar Hotel in 1912.

The National Monument

At the close of the nineteenth century, men such as Join Muir, Gifford Pinchot, and Stephen Mather were pressing for protection of America's natural resources and beauty. Their efforts led President Harrison to set aside the first National Forest Reserves, including Grand Canyon Forest Reserve in 1893. President Theodore Roosevelt was one of the earlier visitors to the Grand Canyon, and his visit helped fuel his growing opinion that the United States needed to preserve places such as Grand Canyon as the common heritage of all the people. In 1908 President Roosevelt proclaimed Grand Canyon National Monument, taking advantage of a new law allowing the president to establish preserves to protect antiquities.

Creating the National Park

Stephen Mather was appointed to head of the newly-formed National Park Service in 1916. Shortly afterward, in 1919, Congress created Grand Canyon National Park and the new park was turned over to the Park Service. Preservation had firmly been established as the management philosophy for the Grand Canyon.

Tourist Camps Below the Rim

Meanwhile, the Santa Fe Railroad was facing difficulties in trying to expand tourism at the South Rim. The only trail to the river from the Grand Canyon Village area was the Bright Angel Trail which was built by a prospector along an old Indian route and operated as a private toll trail. To circumvent this roadblock, the railroad built a road along the rim to Hermits Rest and then built the Hermit Trail to the river. Hermit Camp, an elaborate tourist camp complete with tent cabins, running water, and an aerial tramway for resupply was built near Hermit Creek on the Tonto Platform. Hermit Camp served as the focus for trips into the canyon until 1930.

The Kaibab Trail and Phantom Ranch

The Park Service, frustrated by repeated failures to buy the Bright Angel Trail, finally built its own trail to the east of the village. Construction of both the South and North Kaibab trails required the extensive use of explosives, but when the new trans-canyon trail opened in 1928 it became the focus of tourism below the rim and resulted in the establishment of Phantom Ranch near the mouth of Bright Angel Creek.

Dams

Unfortunately, the national park established in 1919 did not protect all of the Grand Canyon: Marble Canyon, geologically a part of Grand Canyon, and the western portion of the Grand Canyon, were not included. During the 1960's, plans to build two huge dams in the Grand Canyon prompted a national protest. Bridge Canyon Dam in the western Grand Canyon would have flooded part of the park, Marble Canyon Dam would have eliminated the whitewater river run, and the wild heart of the canyon would have been lost. Finally, in 1975, Congress passed a law expanding the park to include all of Marble Canyon and the Grand Canyon except the southwestern portion on the Hualapai and Havasupai Indian reservations. The new law also addressed a long-standing injustice done to the Havasupai Tribe by expanding their reservation to include traditional lands upstream of Supai Village and on the South Rim.

Resources

Maps

Grand Canyon National Park. Bright Angel Canyon and North/South Rim (Trails Illustrated Map, #261)

Grand Canyon National Park, AZ – Trails Illustrated Map #207

TOPO! National Geographic USGS Topographic Maps

National Geographic Heart of the Grand Canyon Map (Grand Canyon National Park, Arizona)

Books

Guidebooks

Grand Canyon National Park Pocket Guide (Falcon Guides)

Hiking Grand Canyon National Park, 2nd (Regional Hiking Series)

Best Easy Day Hikes Grand Canyon, 2nd (Best Easy Day Hikes Series)

Grand Canyon Treks: 12,000 Miles Through the Grand Canyon

Hiking Grand Canyon Loops (Regional Hiking Series)

Day Hikes from the River Third Edition: 100 Hikes from Camps Along the Colorado River in Grand Canyon

Belknap's Waterproof Grand Canyon River Guide All New Edition

Grand Canyon's North Rim and Beyond: A Guide to the North Rim and the Arizona Strip

Geology and Geography

Anatomy of the Grand Canyon: Panoramas of the Canyon's Geology

Grand Canyon Place Names

River to Rim: A Guide to Place Names Along the Colorado River in Grand Canyon from Lake Powell

Carving Grand Canyon: Evidence, Theories, and Mystery

Natural History

Best of Grand Canyon Nature Notes 1926-1935 (Grand Canyon Association)

Human History

Mary Colter: Architect of the Southwest

Sunk Without a Sound : The Tragic Colorado River Honeymoon of Glen and Bessie Hyde

Living at the Edge : Explorers, Exploiters and Settlers of the Grand Canyon Region (Grand Canyon Association)

Over the Edge: Death in Grand Canyon

Narratives

The Exploration of the Colorado River and Its Canyons (Penguin Classics)

The Man Who Walked Through Time: The Story of the First Trip Afoot Through the Grand Canyon

We Swam the Grand Canyon: The True Story of a Cheap Vacation that Got a Little Out of Hand

The Majesty Of The Grand Canyon: 150 Years In Art

Breaking Into the Current: Boatwomen of the Grand Canyon

Grand Obsession: Harvey Butchart and the Exploration of Grand Canyon

Visiting the Grand Canyon: Early Views of Tourism (AZ) (Images of America)

Park Ranger True Stories from a Ranger's Career in America's National Parks

Over the Edge: Death in Grand Canyon

River Runners of the Grand Canyon

A Canyon Voyage: The Narrative of the Second Powell Expedition down the Green-Colorado River from Wyoming, and the Explorations on Land, in the Years 1871 and 1872

Havasu Canyon: Gem of the Grand Canyon--An Illustrated Guide and Information Book About This Scenic and Fascinating Region, the Home of the Havasupai Indians

It Happened at Grand Canyon (It Happened In Series)

Through the Grand Canyon from Wyoming to Mexico (Classic Reprint)

Canyon (Ghiglieri)

There's This River... Grand Canyon Boatman Stories

Grand Canyon Stories: Then & Now

The Incredible Grand Canyon

Summer sojourn to the Grand Canyon: The 1898 diary of Zella Dysart

Art and Photography

Lasting Light: 125 Years of Grand Canyon Photography

Grand Canyon: Views beyond the Beauty

Movies

Grand Canyon Adventure: River at Risk

About the Author

Bruce Grubbs has been hiking, backpacking, and cross-country skiing throughout the American West for more than 40 years. He participated in the technical first ascents of the last major summits to be climbed in the Grand Canyon, including Buddha Temple, Holy Grail Temple, the striking pinnacle at Comanche Point, Malgosa Crest, and Kwagunt Butte. Bruce has spent more than 400 days hiking in the Grand Canyon. He continues to enjoy long backpacking treks in the more remote sections of the Grand Canyon, as well as hiking and backpacking trips elsewhere in the American West.

Outdoor writing and photography have long been serious interests of Bruce's. His first published article was in a local Arizona outdoor magazine 35 years ago, and he has since been published by Backpacker Magazine and several regional publications. About 20 years ago, his writing focus expanded to include books, with the publication of Hiking Arizona with Stewart Aitchison. He has since written twenty-four more published books.

Earlier, Bruce worked eleven seasons as a wildland fire fighter for the U.S. Forest Service and Bureau of Land Management. His positions included fire lookout, engine foreman, helitack foreman, and fire station manager.

He was part owner of an outdoor shop for eight years, selling hiking, backpacking, climbing, and skiing gear. He started and continues to run a successful computer consulting business, offering personal computer support and website design to individual clients and small businesses.

Bruce has been a professional pilot for more than twenty years, and holds an Airline Transport Pilot certificate with multiengine rating. He also holds a Flight Instructor certificate with instrument rating. Currently, he is an active, part-time air charter pilot with more than 7,000 hours of flight time.

Other interests include Amateur Radio, where he served for several years as the Amateur Radio Emergency Coordinator for Coconino County, Arizona. He also is a mountain biker, sea kayaker, and figure skater. He is currently the president of the Flagstaff Figure Skating Club, where he recently helped the club host its first skating competition. He is also the webmaster for the club.

Web Sites

www.GrandCanyonGuide.net

www.BruceGrubbs.com

www.BrightAngelPress.com

www.FlagstaffFigureSkatingClub.com

www.ExploringGPS.com

Blogs

Get Out and Stay Out: Bruce-Grubbs.blogspot.com

TravelsWithKindle.blogspot.com

The author (foreground) and friends on a Grand Canyon summit

Index

CPSIA information can be obtained at www.ICGtesting.com
Printed in the USA
LVOW092144280812

296366LV00027B/172/P